The Trouble with Being Born

BY E. M. CIORAN

Anathemas and Admirations
Drawn and Quartered
History and Utopia
On the Heights of Despair
A Short History of Decay
Tears and Saints
The Temptation to Exist
The Trouble with Being Born

E. M. Cioran

The Trouble with Being Born

Translated from the French by
RICHARD HOWARD

Foreword by
EUGENE THACKER

ARCADE PUBLISHING • NEW YORK

First published in France under the title *De l'inconvénient d'être né*

Arcade Publishing books may be purchased in bulk at special discounts
for sales promotion, corporate gifts, fund-raising, or educational purposes.
Special editions can also be created to specifications. For details, contact
the Special Sales Department, Arcade Publishing, 307 West 36th Street,
11th Floor, New York, NY 10018 or arcade@skyhorsepublishing.com.

Arcade Publishing® is a registered trademark of Skyhorse Publishing, Inc.®,
a Delaware corporation.

Visit our website at www.arcadepub.com.

15 14

Library of Congress Cataloging-in-Publication Data is available on file.

ISBN: 978-1-61145-740-7

Printed in China

Foreword

by Eugene Thacker

In June of 1969, the French newspaper *Le Monde* published a two-page spread entitled "Cioran, or the Contemplative Nihilist." The title was ambiguous; it was difficult to tell if it was meant as an accolade or an accusation. While Cioran's work had been steadily gaining in reputation, many critics and readers were put off by the sullen, morose tone of his books as well as by the difficult-to-categorize style of his writing. To be judged a "contemplative nihilist" is at best a kind of back-handed compliment. The *Le Monde* article may as well have called Cioran a "euphoric pessimist," an equally apt description. It was as if to say, Yes, you may be a nihilist or a pessimist, but only in thought—a nihilist at a distance, a pessimist at arm's length.

When Cioran published *De l'inconvénient d'être né* (translated here as *The Trouble with Being Born*) in 1973, it marked the midpoint of a trajectory that had taken him from a small village in Romania to cosmopolitan Bucharest and then Paris, where he was to remain for the rest of his life. It was a time of loss and refusals for Cioran. A few years before, Cioran's mother and sister had died. A year after the article in *Le Monde*, Cioran's close friend, the playwright Arthur Adamov, committed suicide; less than a year later his colleague, the poet Paul Celan, who had translated Cioran's work into German, also committed suicide; and the year that *The Trouble with Being Born* was published saw the death of another close friend, the existentialist philosopher Gabriel Marcel. It was also a period of refusals.

Cioran proudly spurned several gestures of monetary support, as well as numerous literary prizes, many of them financially significant. All the while Cioran continued to live modestly in his rented apartment on the Rue de l'Odéon, working at his compact and cluttered writing desk, taking his frequent walks in the neighborhood.

In his books, Cioran is always scaling up and zooming out, always posing the question at an even more fundamental level, and it is this approach that characterizes *The Trouble with Being Born*. Here we see Cioran grappling with an age-old philosophical dilemma—the problem with being here, in this moment, thrown into an existence that one has neither asked for nor desired, in a world that we have difficulty wholeheartedly accepting or rejecting. Today, in the early years of the new millennium, academics discuss the problems of global climate change, sustainability, and overpopulation, taking sides in philosophical debates on natalism and antinatalism. Such debates are not new. In the 1970s, journalists and public thinkers frequently discussed the "population bomb" and the "end of history." But in *The Trouble with Being Born* Cioran remains skeptical of such a myopic emphasis on the present—his writing asks whether such issues are not simply an indicator of a fraught relationship to our own mortality—the latest stage in Western culture's "fall into time." It is hard not to see *The Trouble with Being Born* as an extended meditation on the problem of time and temporality that begins with Cioran's own devastating realization late one night, in the slow seconds of his lifelong struggle with insomnia: "Three in the morning. I realize this second, then this one, then the next: I draw up a balance sheet for each minute. And why all this? *Because I was born*. It is a special type of sleeplessness that produces the indictment of birth."

The content of *The Trouble with Being Born* is inseparable from its form. This is a hallmark of every one of Cioran's books, but *The Trouble with Being Born* is unique in Cioran's oeuvre in that it is rigorously composed entirely of brief and concise aphorisms. It is here that Cioran's influences are the most apparent, particularly that of the tradition of the philosophical aphorism—Chamfort, La Rochefoucauld, Leopardi, Novalis, Nietzsche. In its style, it looks back to Cioran's books such as *All Gall Is Divided* and forward to *Drawn and Quartered*. But *The Trouble with Being Born* is the most uncompromising of the lot, at once an extended meditation on the problems of temporal contingency and yet an unfinished scattering of chance thoughts and anxious epiphanies. Each of the aphorisms touches the reader with a certain immaterial weight, like a slow clock ticking off one second after the other. Even the French title, *De l'inconvénient d'être né,* betrays this profound hesitancy—literally, "On the inconvenience of having been born"—a phrase at once sardonic and tragic, a combination emblematic of Cioran's twilight thought.

The Trouble with Being Born

1

Three in the morning. I realize this second, then this one, then the next: I draw up the balance sheet for each minute. And why all this? *Because I was born.* It is a special type of sleeplessness that produces the indictment of birth.

§

"Ever since I was born"—that *since* has a resonance so dreadful to my ears it becomes unendurable.

§

There is a kind of knowledge that strips whatever you do of weight and scope: for such knowledge, everything is without basis except itself. Pure to the point of abhorring even the notion of an object, it translates that extreme science according to which doing or not doing something comes down to the same thing and is accompanied by an equally extreme satisfaction: that of being able to rehearse, each time, the discovery that any gesture performed is not worth defending, that nothing is enhanced by the merest vestige of substance, that "reality" falls within the province of lunacy. Such knowledge deserves to be called posthumous: it functions as if the knower were alive and not alive, a being and the memory of a being. "It's already in the past," he says about all he achieves, even as he achieves it, thereby forever destitute of the *present.*

§

We do not rush toward death, we flee the catastrophe of birth, survivors struggling to forget it. Fear of death is merely the projection into the future of a fear which dates back to our first moment of life.

We are reluctant, of course, to treat birth as a scourge: has it not been inculcated as the sovereign good—have we not been told that the worst came at the end, not at the outset of our lives? Yet evil, the real evil, is *behind*, not ahead of us. What escaped Jesus did not escape Buddha: "If three things did not exist in the world, O disciples, the Perfect One would not appear in the world. . . ." And ahead of old age and death he places the fact of birth, source of every infirmity, every disaster.

§

We can endure any truth, however destructive, provided it replaces everything, provided it affords as much vitality as the hope for which it substitutes.

§

I do nothing, granted. But I *see* the hours pass—which is better than trying to fill them.

§

No need to elaborate *works*—merely say something that can be murmured in the ear of a drunkard or a dying man.

§

Nothing is a better proof of how far humanity has regressed than the impossibility of finding a single nation, a single tribe, among whom birth still provokes mourning and lamentations.

§

To defy heredity is to defy billions of years, to defy the *first* cell.

§

There is a god at the outset, if not at the end, of every joy.

§

Never comfortable in the immediate, I am lured only by what precedes me, what distances me from here, the numberless moments when I was not: the non-born.

§

Physical need of dishonor. How I should have liked to be the executioner's son!

§

What right have you to pray for me? I need no intercessor, I shall manage *alone*. The prayers of a wretch I might accept, but no one else's, not even a saint's. I cannot bear your bothering about my salvation. If I apprehend salvation and flee it, your prayers are merely an indiscretion. Invest them elsewhere; in any case, we do not serve the same gods. If mine are impotent, there is every reason to believe yours are no less so. Even assuming they are as you imagine them, they would still lack the power to cure me of a horror older than my memory.

§

What misery a sensation is! Ecstasy itself, *perhaps*, is nothing more.

§

Unmaking, decreating, is the only task man may take upon himself, if he aspires, as everything suggests, to distinguish himself from the Creator.

§

I know that my birth is fortuitous, a laughable accident, and yet, as soon as I forget myself, I behave as if it were a capital event, indispensable to the progress and equilibrium of the world.

§

To have committed every crime but that of being a father.

§

As a general rule, men *expect* disappointment: they know they must not be impatient, that it will come sooner or later, that it will hold off long enough for them to proceed with their undertakings of the moment. The disabused man is different: for him, disappointment occurs at the same time as the deed; he has no need to await it, it is present. By freeing himself from succession, he has devoured the possible and rendered the future superfluous. "I cannot meet you in *your* future," he says to the others. "We do not have a single moment in common." Because for him the whole of the future is already here.

When we perceive the end in the beginning, we move faster than time. Illumination, that lightning disappointment, affords a certitude which transforms disillusion into deliverance.

§

I disentangle myself from appearances, yet I am snarled in them nonetheless; or rather: I am halfway between these appearances and *that* which invalidates them, *that* which has neither name nor content, *that* which is nothing and everything. I shall never take the decisive step outside them; my nature forces me to drift, to remain forever in the equivocal, and if I were to attempt a clean break in one direction or the other, I should perish by my salvation.

§

My faculty for disappointment surpasses understanding. It is what lets me comprehend Buddha, but also what keeps me from following him.

§

What we can no longer commiserate with counts for nothing— no longer exists. We realize why our past so quickly stops being "ours" and turns into history, something which no longer concerns anyone.

§

In the deepest part of yourself, aspire to be as dispossessed, as lamentable as God.

§

True contact between beings is established only by mute presence, by apparent non-communication, by that mysterious and wordless exchange which resembles inward prayer.

§

What I know at sixty, I knew as well at twenty. Forty years of a long, a superfluous, labor of verification.

§

I am for the most part so convinced that everything is lacking in basis, consequence, justification, that if someone dared to contradict me, even the man I most admire, he would seem to me a charlatan or a fool.

§

Even in childhood I watched the hours flow, independent of any reference, any action, any event, the disjunction of time from what was not itself, its autonomous existence, its special status, its empire, its tyranny. I remember quite clearly that afternoon when, for the first time, confronting the empty universe, I was no more than a passage of moments reluctant to go on playing their proper parts. Time was coming unstuck from being—*at my expense.*

§

Unlike Job, I have not cursed the day I was born; all the other days, on the contrary, I have covered with my anathemas. . . .

§

If death had only negative aspects, dying would be an unmanageable action.

§

Everything exists; nothing exists. Either formula affords a like serenity. The man of anxiety, to his misfortune, remains between them, trembling and perplexed, forever at the mercy of a nuance, incapable of gaining a foothold in the security of being or in the absence of being.

§

Here on the coast of Normandy, at this hour of the morning, I needed no one. The very gulls' presence bothered me: I drove them off with stones. And hearing their supernatural shrieks, I realized that that was just what I wanted, that only the Sinister could soothe me, and that it was for such a confrontation that I had got up before dawn.

§

"In this our life"—*to be in life:* suddenly I am struck by the strangeness of such an expression, as if it applied to no one.

§

Whenever I flag and feel sorry for my brain, I am carried away by an irresistible desire to *proclaim.* That is the moment I realize the paltry depths out of which rise reformers, prophets, and saviors.

§

I long to be free—desperately free. Free as the stillborn are free.

§

If there is so much discomfort and ambiguity in lucidity, it is because lucidity is the result of the poor use to which we have put our sleepless nights.

§

Our obsession with birth, by shifting us to a point *before* our past, robs us of our pleasure in the future, in the present, and even in the past.

§

Rare are the days when, projected into post-history, I fail to witness the gods' hilarity at leaving behind the human episode.

What we need is an alternate vision, when that of the Last Judgment no longer satisfies anyone.

§

An idea, a being, anything which becomes incarnate loses identity, turns grotesque. Frustration of all achievement. Never quit the possible, wallow in eternal trifling, *forget* to be born.

§

The real, the unique misfortune: to see the light of day. A disaster which dates back to aggressiveness, to the seed of expansion and rage within origins, to the tendency to the worst which first shook them up.

§

When we see someone again after many years, we should sit down facing each other and say nothing for hours, so that by means of silence our consternation can relish itself.

§

Days of miraculous sterility. Instead of rejoicing over them, proclaiming victory, transforming this drought into a celebration, seeing it as an illustration of my fulfillment, my maturity, in short my detachment, I let myself be invaded by spite and resentment: so tenacious is the old Adam in us, the bustling *canaille,* unfit for self-effacement.

§

I am enraptured by Hindu philosophy, whose essential endeavor is to surmount the self; and everything I do, everything I think is only myself and the self's humiliations.

§

While we are performing an action, we have a goal; performed, the action has no more reality for us than the goal we were seeking. Nothing of much consequence here—no more than a game. But some of us are conscious of this game *in the course of* the action: we experience the conclusion in the premises, the achieved in the virtual—we undermine "seriousness" by the very fact that we exist.

The vision of non-reality, of universal default, is the product of an everyday sensation and a sudden *frisson. Everything is a game*—without such a revelation, the sensation we haul through our usual lives would not have that characteristic stamp our metaphysical experiences require to be distinguished from their imitations, our *discomforts*. For every discomfort is only an abortive metaphysical experience.

§

When we have worn out the interest we once took in death, when we realize we have nothing more to gain from it, we fall back on birth, we turn to a much more inexhaustible abyss.

§

At this very moment, I am suffering—as we say in French, *j'ai mal*. This event, crucial for me, is nonexistent, even inconceivable for anyone else, for everyone else. Except for God, if that word can have a meaning.

§

We hear on all sides, that if everything is pointless, to do well whatever it is you're doing is not. Yet it is, even so. To reach this conclusion, and to endure it, you need ply no trade, or at most, a king's—say, Solomon's.

§

I react like everyone else, even like those I most despise; but I make up for it by deploring every action I commit, good or bad.

§

Where are my sensations? They have melted into . . . me, and what is this me, this self, but the sum of these evaporated sensations?

§

Extraordinary and *null*—these two adjectives apply to the sexual act, and, consequently, to everything resulting from it, to life first of all.

§

Lucidity is the only vice which makes us free—free *in a desert.*

§

As the years pass, the number of those we can communicate with diminishes. When there is no longer anyone to talk to, at last we will be as we were before stooping to a name.

§

Once we reject lyricism, to blacken a page becomes an ordeal: what's the use of writing in order to say *exactly* what we had to say?

§

We cannot consent to be judged by someone who has suffered less than ourselves. And since each of us regards himself as an unrecognized Job . . .

§

I dream of an ideal confessor to tell everything to, spill it all: I dream of a blasé saint.

§

After all the ages of dying, the living must have learned the trick; how else explain how the insect, the rodent, and man himself have managed, after a little fuss, to do it so properly?

§

Paradise was unendurable, otherwise the first man would have adapted to it; this world is no less so, since here we regret paradise or anticipate another one. What to do? where to go? Do nothing and go nowhere, easy enough.

§

Health is certainly a good thing; but those who possess it have been denied the opportunity of realizing it, for self-conscious health is either compromised or about to be. Since no one delights in his absence of infirmities, we may speak without exaggeration of a *just* punishment of the healthy.

§

Some have misfortunes; others, obsessions. Which are worse off?

§

Don't be fair to me: I can do without everything but the tonic of injustice.

§

"All is suffering"—modernized, the Buddhist expression runs: "All is nightmare."

Thereby, nirvana, whose mission now is to end a much more widespread torment, is no longer a recourse reserved to the few but becomes as universal as nightmare itself.

§

What is that one crucifixion compared to the daily kind any insomniac endures?

§

I was walking late one night along a tree-lined path; a chestnut fell at my feet. The noise it made as it burst, the resonance it provoked in me, and an upheaval out of all proportion to this insignificant event thrust me into miracle, into the rapture of the definitive, as if there were no more questions—only answers. I was drunk on a thousand unexpected discoveries, none of which I could make use of. . . .

This is how I nearly reached the Supreme. But instead I went on with my walk.

§

We tell our troubles to someone only to make him suffer, to make him assume them for himself. If we wanted to win him over, we would admit none but abstract worries, the only kind those who love us are eager to hear.

§

I do not forgive myself for being born. It is as if, creeping into this world, I had profaned a mystery, betrayed some momentous pledge, committed a fault of nameless gravity. Yet in a less assured mood, birth seems a calamity I would be miserable not having known.

§

Thought is never *innocent*, for it is pitiless, it is aggressive, it helps us burst our bonds. Were we to suppress what is evil and even demonic in thought, we should have to renounce the very concept of deliverance.

§

The surest way of not being deceived is to undermine one certainty after the next. Yet the fact remains that everything that matters was accomplished *outside* doubt.

§

For a long time—always, in fact—I have known that life here on earth is not what I needed and that I wasn't able to deal with it; for this reason and for this reason alone, I have acquired a touch of spiritual pride, so that my existence seems to me the degradation and the erosion of a psalm.

§

Our thoughts, in the pay of our panic, are oriented toward the future, follow the trail of all fear, open out onto death. And we invert their course, we send them backward when we direct them toward birth and force them to linger upon it. Thereby they lose even that vigor, that unappeasable tension which underlies the horror of death and which is useful to our thoughts if they would grow, develop, gather force. Hence we see why, by taking a contrary trajectory, they lack spirit and are so weary, when at last they come up against their initial frontier, that they no longer have the energy to look beyond, toward the "never-born."

§

It is not my beginnings, it is the beginning that matters to me. If I bump into my birth, into a minor obsession, it is because I cannot grapple with the first moment of time. Every individual discomfort leads back, ultimately, to a cosmogonic discomfort, each of our sensations expiating that crime of the primordial sensation, by which Being crept out of somewhere. . . .

§

Though we may prefer ourselves to the universe, we nonetheless loathe ourselves much more than we suspect. If the wise man is so rare a phenomenon, it is because he seems unshaken by the aversion which, like all beings, he must feel for himself.

§

No difference between being and non-being, if we apprehend them with the same intensity.

§

Nescience is the basis of everything, it creates everything by an action repeated every moment, it produces this and any world, since it continually takes for real what in fact is not. Nescience is the tremendous mistake that serves as the basis of all our truths, it is older and more powerful than all the gods combined.

§

This is how we recognize the man who has tendencies toward an inner quest: he will set failure above any success, he will even seek it out, unconsciously of course. This is because failure, always *essential*, reveals us to ourselves, permits us to see ourselves as God sees us, whereas success distances us from what is most inward in ourselves and indeed in everything.

§

There was a time when time did not yet exist. . . . The rejection of birth is nothing but the nostalgia for this time before time.

§

I think of so many friends who are no more, and I pity them. Yet they are not so much to be pitied, for they have solved every problem, beginning with the problem of death.

§

In the fact of being born there is such an absence of necessity that when you think about it a little more than usual, you are left—ignorant how to react—with a foolish grin.

§

Two kinds of mind: daylight and nocturnal. They have neither the same method nor the same morality. In broad daylight, you watch yourself; in the dark, you speak out. The salutary or awkward consequences of what he thinks matter little to the man who questions himself at hours when others are the prey of sleep. Hence he meditates upon the bad luck of being born without concern for the harm he can cause others or himself. After midnight begins the intoxication of pernicious truths.

§

As the years accumulate, we form an increasingly somber image of the future. Is this only to console ourselves for being excluded from it? Yes in appearance, no in fact, for the future has always been hideous, man being able to remedy his evils only by aggravating them, so that in each epoch existence is much more tolerable before the solution is found to the difficulties of the moment.

§

In major perplexities, try to live as if history were done with and to react like a monster riddled by serenity.

§

If I used to ask myself, over a coffin: "What good did it do the occupant to be born?", I now put the same question about anyone alive.

§

The emphasis on birth is no more than the craving for the insoluble carried to the point of insanity.

§

Regarding death, I ceaselessly waver between "mystery" and "inconsequentiality"—between the Pyramids and the Morgue.

§

It is impossible to *feel* that there was a time when we did not exist. Hence our attachment to the personage we were before being born.

§

"Meditate but one hour upon the self's nonexistence and you will feel yourself to be another man," said a priest of the Japanese Kusha sect to a Western visitor.

Without having frequented the Buddhist monasteries, how many times have I not lingered over the world's unreality, and hence my own? I have not become another man for that, no, but there certainly has remained with me the feeling that my identity is entirely illusory, and that by losing it I have lost nothing, except something, except *everything*.

§

Instead of clinging to the fact of being born, as good sense bids, I take the risk, I turn back, I retrogress increasingly toward some unknown beginning, I move from origin to origin. Some day, perhaps, I shall manage to reach origin itself, in order to rest there, or be wrecked.

§

X insults me. I am about to hit him. Thinking it over, I refrain.

Who am I? which is my real self: the self of the retort or that of the refraining? My first reaction is always energetic; the second one, flabby. What is known as "wisdom" is ultimately only a perpetual "thinking it over," i.e., non-action as first impulse.

§

If attachment is an evil, we must look for its cause in the scandal of birth, for to be born is to be attached. Detachment then should apply itself to getting rid of the traces of this scandal, the most serious and intolerable of all.

§

Amid anxiety and distress, sudden calm at the thought of the foetus one has been.

§

At this precise moment, no reproach proceeding from men or gods can affect me: I have as good a conscience as if I had never existed.

§

It is a mistake to believe in a direct relation between suffering reverses and being dead set against birth. Such opposition has deeper, more distant roots, and would occur even if one had only the shadow of a grievance against existence. In fact it is never more virulent than in cases of extreme good fortune.

§

Thracians and Bogomils—I cannot forget that I have haunted the same whereabouts as they, nor that the former wept over the newborn and the latter, in order to justify God, held Satan responsible for the infamy of Creation.

§

During the long nights in the caves, how many Hamlets must have murmured their endless monologues—for it is likely that the apogee of metaphysical torment is to be located well before that universal insipidity which followed the advent of Philosophy.

§

The obsession with birth proceeds from an exacerbation of memory, from an omnipresence of the past, as well as from a craving for the impasse, for the *first* impasse. —No openness, hence no joy from the past but solely from the present, and from a future *emancipated from time.*

§

For years, in fact for life, to have meditated only on your last moments, only to discover, when at last you approach them, that it was of no use, that the thought of death helps in everything save in dying!

§

It is our discomforts which provoke, which create consciousness; their task accomplished, they weaken and disappear one after the other. Consciousness however remains and survives them, without recalling what it owes to them, without even ever having known. Hence it continually proclaims its autonomy, its sovereignty, even when it loathes itself and would do away with itself.

§

According to the Rule of Saint Benedict, if a monk became proud of or merely satisfied with the task he was performing, he was to forsake it then and there.

One danger not dreaded by the man who has lived in the thirst for unsatisfaction, in an orgy of remorse and disgust.

§

If it is true that God dislikes taking sides, I should feel no awkwardness in His presence, so pleased would I be to imitate Him, to be like Him, in everything, "without opinion."

§

To get up in the morning, wash and then wait for some unforeseen variety of dread or depression.

I would give the whole universe and all of Shakespeare for a grain of ataraxy.

§

Nietzsche's great luck—to have ended as he did: in euphoria!

§

Endlessly to refer to a world where nothing yet stooped to occurrence, where you anticipated consciousness without desiring it, where, wallowing in the virtual, you rejoiced in the null plenitude of a self anterior to selfhood. . . .

Not to have been born, merely musing on that—what happiness, what freedom, what space!

2

If disgust for the world conferred sanctity of itself, I fail to see how I could avoid canonization.

§

No one has lived so close to his skeleton as I have lived to mine: from which results an endless dialogue and certain truths which I manage neither to accept nor to reject.

§

It is easier to *get on* with vices than with virtues. The vices, accommodating by nature, help each other, are full of mutual indulgence, whereas the jealous virtues combat and annihilate each other, showing in everything their incompatibility and their intolerance.

§

It is trifling to believe in what you do or in what others do. You should avoid simulacra and even "realities"; you should take up a position external to everything and everyone, drive off or grind down your appetites, live, according to a Hindu adage, with as few desires as a "solitary elephant."

§

I forgive X everything because of his obsolete smile.

§

He who hates himself is not humble.

§

In certain men, everything, absolutely everything, derives from physiology: their body is their mind, their mind is their body.

§

Time, fertile in resources, more inventive and more charitable than we think, possesses a remarkable capacity to help us out, to afford us at any hour of the day some new humiliation.

§

I have always sought out landscapes that preceded God. Whence my weakness for Chaos.

§

I have decided not to oppose anyone ever again, since I have noticed that I always end by resembling my latest enemy.

§

For a long while I have lived with the notion that I was the most normal being that ever existed. This notion gave me the taste, even the passion for being unproductive: what was the use of being prized in a world inhabited by madmen, a world mired in mania and stupidity? For whom was one to bother, and to what end? It remains to be seen if I have quite freed myself from this certitude, salvation in the absolute, ruin in the immediate.

§

Violent men are generally sickly, "broken-down." They live in perpetual combustion, at the expense of their bodies, exactly like ascetics, who in the discipline of quietude erode and exhaust themselves, quite as much as the furious.

§

Write books only if you are going to say in them the things you would never dare confide to anyone.

§

When Mara, the Tempter, tries to supplant the Buddha, the latter says, among other things: "By what right do you claim to rule over men and over the universe? *Have you suffered for knowledge?*"

This is the crucial, perhaps the sole question we should ask ourselves when we scrutinize anything, especially a thinker. There is never too great a distinction made between those who have paid for the tiniest step toward knowledge and those, incomparably more numerous, who have received a convenient, indifferent knowledge, a knowledge *without ordeals*.

§

We say: he has no talent, only tone. But tone is precisely what cannot be invented—we're born with it. Tone is an inherited grace, the privilege some of us have of making our organic pulsations felt—tone is more than talent, it is its essence.

§

The same feeling of not belonging, of futility, wherever I go: I pretend interest in what matters nothing to me, I bestir myself mechanically or out of charity, without ever being caught up, without ever being somewhere. What attracts me is elsewhere, and I don't know what that elsewhere is.

§

The farther men get from God, the farther they advance into the knowledge of religions.

§

"For God doth know that in the day ye eat thereof, then your eyes shall be opened. . . ."

No sooner are they open than the drama begins. To look *without understanding*—that is paradise. Hell, then, would be the place where we understand, where we understand too much. . . .

§

I get along quite well with someone only when he is at his lowest point and has neither the desire nor the strength to restore his habitual illusions.

§

Pitilessly judging our contemporaries, we have every likelihood of figuring, in the eyes of posterity, as penetrating minds. At one stroke we renounce the risky aspect of admiration, the marvelous perils it supposes. For admiration is a risk, the most unforeseeable of all because it may happen to turn out well.

§

Ideas come as you walk, Nietzsche said. Walking dissipates thoughts, Shankara taught.

Both theses are equally well-founded, hence equally true, as each of us can discover for himself in the space of an hour, sometimes of a minute. . . .

§

No variety of literary originality is still possible unless we torture, unless we pulverize language. It proceeds differently if we abide by the expression of the idea as such. Here we find ourselves in an area where requirements have not altered since the pre-Socratics.

§

If only we could reach back before the concept, could write on a level with the senses, record the infinitesimal variations of what we touch, do what a reptile would do if it were to set about writing!

§

Anything good we can have comes from our indolence, from our incapability of taking action, executing our projects and plans. It is the impossibility or the refusal of self-realization which sustains our "virtues," and it is the will to do our utmost that carries us to excesses, to disorders.

§

That "glorious delirium" Saint Teresa of Ávila speaks of, invoking one of the phases of her union with God, is what a desiccated mind, necessarily jealous, will never forgive the mystics.

§

Not one moment when I have not been conscious of being outside Paradise.

§

Only what you hide is profound, is true. Whence the power of base feelings.

§

Ama nesciri, says the *Imitation of Christ*. Love to be unknown. We are happy with ourselves and with the world only when we conform to this precept.

§

The intrinsic value of a book does not depend on the importance of its subject (else the theologians would prevail, and mightily), but on the manner of approaching the accidental and the insignificant, of mastering the infinitesimal. The *essential* has never required the least talent.

§

The feeling of being ten thousand years behind, or ahead, of the others, of belonging to the beginnings or to the end of humanity . . .

§

Negation never proceeds from reasoning but from something much more obscure and old. Arguments come afterward, to justify and sustain it. Every *no* rises out of the blood.

§

With the help of the erosion of memory, to *recall* the first initiatives of matter and the risk of life which followed from them . . .

§

Each time I fail to think about death, I have the impression of cheating, of deceiving someone in me.

§

There are nights that the most ingenious torturers could not have invented. We emerge from them in pieces, stupid, dazed, with neither memories nor anticipations, and without even knowing who we are. And it is then that the day seems useless, light pernicious, even more oppressive than the darkness.

§

A *conscious* fruit fly would have to confront exactly the same difficulties, the same kind of insoluble problems as man.

§

Better to be an animal than a man, an insect than an animal, a plant than an insect, and so on.

Salvation? Whatever diminishes the kingdom of consciousness and compromises its supremacy.

§

I have all the defects of other people and yet everything they do seems to me inconceivable.

§

Considering things according to nature, man was made to live facing outward. If he would see into himself, he must close his eyes, renounce his endeavors, quit the immediate. What is called "inner life" is a belated phenomenon, possible only by a slowing down of our vital activities, "the soul" being able to emerge and elaborate itself only at the expense of the good behavior of our organs.

§

The merest atmospheric variation jeopardizes my plans, not to speak of my convictions. This kind of dependency—the most humiliating kind—unfailingly lays me low, even as it dissipates what few illusions remain as to my possibilities of being free and as to freedom itself. What is the use of swaggering if you are at the mercy of Wet and Dry? One craves a less lamentable bondage, and gods of another kidney.

§

It's not worth the bother of killing yourself, since you always kill yourself *too late*.

§

When you know quite absolutely that everything is unreal, you then cannot see why you should take the trouble to prove it.

§

As it leaves dawn behind and advances into the day, light prostitutes itself and is redeemed—ethics of twilight—only at the moment it vanishes.

§

In Buddhist writings, mention is often made of "the abyss of birth." An abyss indeed, a gulf into which we do not fall but from which, instead, we emerge, to our universal chagrin.

§

At increasingly wider intervals, impulses of gratitude toward Job and Chamfort—toward vociferation and vitriol . . .

§

Each opinion, each view is necessarily partial, truncated, inadequate. In philosophy and in an,thing, originality comes down to incomplete definitions.

§

If we consider closely our so-called generous actions, there is none which,, from some aspect, is not blameworthy and even harmful, so that we come to regret having performed it—so that we must choose, finally, between abstention and remorse.

§

Explosive force of any mortification. Every vanquished desire affords us power. We have the more hold over this world the further we withdraw from it, the less we adhere to it. Renunciation confers an infinite power.

§

My disappointments, instead of converging toward a center and constituting if not a system at least an ensemble, are scattered, each supposing itself unique and thereby wasted, lacking organization.

§

The only successful philosophies and religions are the ones that flatter us, whether in the name of progress or of hell. Damned or not, man experiences an absolute need to be at the heart of everything. It is, in fact, solely for this reason that he is man, that he has *become* man. And if some day he no longer feels this need, he must give way to some other animal prouder, madder than himself.

§

He detested objective truths, the burden of argument, sustained reasoning. He disliked demonstrating, he wanted to convince no one. *Others* are a dialectician's invention.

§

The more injured you are by time, the more you seek to escape it. To write a faultless page, or only a sentence, raises you above becoming and its corruptions. You transcend death by the pursuit of the indestructible in speech, in the very symbol of nullity.

§

At the climax of a failure, at the moment when shame is about to do us in, suddenly we are swept away by a frenzy of pride which lasts only long enough to drain us, to leave us without energy, to lower, with our powers, the intensity of our shame.

§

If death is as horrible as is claimed, how is it that after the passage of a certain period of time we consider *happy* any being, friend or enemy, who has ceased to live?

§

More than once, I have managed to leave my room, for if I had stayed there I could not be sure of being able to resist some *sudden* resolution. The street is more reassuring, you think less about yourself there, there everything weakens and wilts, beginning with your own confusion.

§

Characteristic of sickness to stay awake when everything sleeps, when everything is at rest, even the sick man.

§

When we are young, we take a certain pleasure in our infirmities. They seem so new, so rich! With age, they no longer surprise us, we know them too well. Now, without anything unexpected in them, they do not deserve to be endured.

§

Once we appeal to our most intimate selves, once we begin to labor and to produce, we lay claim to gifts, we become unconscious of our own gaps. No one is in a position to admit that what comes out of his own depths might be worthless. "Self-knowledge"? A contradiction in terms.

§

All these poems where it is merely the Poem that is in question—a whole poetry with no other substance than itself! What would we say of a prayer whose object was religion?

§

The mind that puts everything in question reaches, after a thousand interrogations, an almost total inertia, a situation which the inert, in fact, knows from the start, by instinct. For what is inertia but a congenital perplexity?

§

What a disappointment that Epicurus, the sage I most need, should have written over three hundred treatises! And what a relief that they are lost!

§

"What do you do from morning to night?"
"I endure myself."

§

A remark of my brother's apropos of the troubles and pains our mother endured: "Old age is nature's self-criticism."

§

"One must be mad or drunk," the Abbé Sieyès said, to speak well in the known languages. One must be drunk or mad, I should add, to dare, still, to use words, any word. . . .

§

The fanatic of elliptical gloom is sure to excel in any career save that of being a writer.

§

Having always lived in fear of being surprised by the worst, I have tried in every circumstance to get a head start, flinging myself into misfortune long before it occurred.

§

We do not envy those who have the capacity to pray, whereas we are filled with envy of the possessors of goods, of those who know wealth and fame. Strange that we resign ourselves to someone's salvation and not to what fugitive advantages he may enjoy.

§

I never met one *interesting* mind that was not richly endowed with inadmissible deficiencies.

§

No true art without a strong dose of banality. The constant employment of the unaccustomed readily wearies us, nothing being more unendurable than the uniformity of the exceptional.

§

The trouble with using a borrowed language is that you have no right to make too many mistakes in it. Now, it is by seeking a certain incorrectness without however abusing it, it is by continually approaching solecism, that writing may be given the appearance of life.

§

Each of us believes, quite unconsciously of course, that he alone pursues the truth, which the rest are incapable of seeking out and unworthy of attaining. This madness is so deep-rooted and so useful that it is impossible to realize what would become of each of us if it were someday to disappear.

§

The first thinker was, without a doubt, the first man obsessed by *why*. An unaccustomed mania, not at all contagious: rare indeed are those who suffer from it, who are a prey to questioning, and who can accept no *given* because they were born in consternation.

§

To be objective is to treat others as you treat an object, a corpse—to behave with them like an undertaker.

§

This very second has vanished forever, lost in the anonymous mass of the irrevocable. It will never return. I suffer from this, and I do not. Everything is unique—and insignificant.

§

Emily Brontë: everything that comes from *her* has the capacity to overwhelm me. Haworth is my Mecca.

§

To walk along a stream, to pass, to flow with the water, without effort, without haste, while death continues in us its ruminations, its uninterrupted soliloquy . . . .

§

Only God has the privilege of abandoning us. Men can only drop us.

§

Without the faculty of forgetting, our past would weigh so heavily on our present that we should not have the strength to confront another moment, still less to live through it. Life would be bearable only to frivolous natures, those in fact who do not remember.

§

Plotinus, Porphyry tells us, had the gift of reading men's souls. One day, without any warning, he told his astounded disciple not to try killing himself but rather to take a journey. Porphyry left for Sicily: there he was cured of his melancholy but, he adds regretfully, he thereby missed being present at his master's death, which occurred during his absence.

It has been a long time since philosophers have read men's souls. It is not their task, we are told. Perhaps. But we must not be surprised if they no longer matter much to us.

§

A work exists only if it is elaborated in the darkness with attention, with all the care of the murderer plotting his crime. In both cases, what counts is the will to *strike*.

§

Self-knowledge—the bitterest knowledge of all and also the kind we cultivate least: what is the use of catching ourselves out, morning to night, in the act of illusion, pitilessly tracing each act back to its root, and losing case after case before our own tribunal?

§

Each time I have a lapse of memory, I think of the anguish which must afflict those who *know* they no longer remember anything. But something tells me that after a certain time a secret joy possesses them, a joy they would not agree to trade for any of their memories, even the most stirring. . . .

§

To claim you are more detached, more alien to everything than anyone, and to be merely a fanatic of indifference!

§

The more you are a victim of contradictory impulses, the less you know which to yield to. *To lack character*—precisely that and nothing but.

§

Pure time, time decanted, freed of events, beings, and things, appears only at certain moments of the night, when you feel it coming on, with the one intention of sweeping you off toward an exemplary catastrophe.

3

Suddenly feeling that you know as much as God about anything and everything and quite as suddenly seeing this sensation vanish . . .

§

Firsthand thinkers meditate upon things; the others upon problems. We must live face to face with being, and not with the mind.

§

"What are you waiting for in order to give up?" —Each sickness sends us a summons disguised as a question. We play deaf, even as we realize that the game is played out and that next time we must have the courage, at last, to capitulate.

§

The older I grow, the less I react to frenzy, delirium. My taste, among thinkers, now goes only to extinct volcanoes.

§

As a young man, I bored myself to death, but I believed in myself. If I had no suspicion of the dreary creature I was to become, I knew nonetheless that, whatever happened, Perplexity would not desert me, that it would keep watch over my years with all the zeal and exactitude of Providence.

§

If we could see ourselves as others see us, we would vanish on the spot.

§

I once remarked to an Italian friend that the Latin peoples are *without secrecy*—too open, too garrulous—and that I preferred nations ravaged by timidity, adding that a writer who has failed to know it in his life is worthless in his writings. "You're right," he answered. "When we describe our experiences in our books, there is a lack of intensity, and of extension, for we have already told them a hundred times before." Whereupon we talked about the literature of femininity, of its absence of mystery in countries where the salon and the confessional prevail.

§

We should never deprive ourselves, I forget who once remarked, of the "pleasures of piety." Has religion ever been justified more delicately?

§

This craving to revise our enthusiasms, to change idols, to pray *elsewhere* . . .

§

To stretch out in a field, to smell the earth and tell yourself it is the end as well as the hope of our dejections, that it would be futile to search for anything better to rest on, to dissolve into. . . .

§

When I happen to be busy, I never give a moment's thought to the "meaning" of anything, particularly of whatever it is I am doing. A proof that the secret of everything is in action and not in abstention, that fatal cause of consciousness.

§

What will be the physiognomy of painting, of poetry, of music, in a hundred years? No one can tell. As after the fall of Athens, of Rome, a long pause will intervene, caused by the exhaustion of the means of expression, as well as by the exhaustion of consciousness itself. Humanity, to rejoin the past, must invent a second naïveté, without which the arts can never begin again.

§

In one of the chapels of this ideally ugly church, we find the Virgin standing with her Son above the globe: an aggressive sect which has undermined and conquered an empire and inherited its flaws, beginning with gigantism.

§

It is written in the Zohar: "When man appeared, thereupon appeared the flowers." I suspect they were there long before him, and that his advent plunged them all into a stupefaction from which they have not yet recovered.

§

Impossible to read a line by Kleist without thinking that he committed suicide: as if his suicide had preceded his works.

§

In the Orient, the oddest, the most idiosyncratic Western thinkers would never have been taken seriously, on account of their contradictions. This is precisely why we are interested in them. We prefer not a mind but the reversals, the *biography* of a mind, the incompatibilities and aberrations to be found there, in short those thinkers who, unable to conform to the rest of humanity and still less to themselves, cheat as much by whim as by fatality. Their distinctive sign? A touch of fakery in the tragic, a hint of dalliance even in the irremediable.

§

If, in her *Foundations*, Teresa of Avila lingers over the subject of melancholia, it is because she recognizes it as incurable. Physicians, she says, cannot deal with it, and the mother superior of a convent, faced with such sufferers, has but one recourse: to inspire them with the dread of authority, to threaten them, to frighten them. The saint's method remains the best: only kicks, slaps, and a good beating will be effective in the case of a "depressive." Moreover, such treatment is precisely what the "depressive" himself resorts to when he decides to end it all: he merely employs more thorough means.

§

In relation to any act of life, the mind acts as a killjoy.

§

Easy to imagine the elements, bored with their exhausted theme, disgusted by their invariable and utterly predictable combinations, seeking some diversion: life would be merely a digression, merely an anecdote. . . .

§

Anything that can be *done* seems to me pernicious and at best futile. If need be I can rouse myself but not act. I understand all too well Wordsworth's description of Coleridge: *eternal activity without action.*

§

Whenever something still seems possible, I have the sense I have been bewitched.

§

The one sincere confession is the one we make indirectly—when we talk about other people.

§

We do not adopt a belief because it is true (they are all true), but because some obscure power impels us to do so. When this power leaves us, we suffer prostration and collapse, a tête-à-tête with what is left of ourselves.

§

"The quality of every perfect form is to release the mind immediately, whereas the corrupt form holds the mind prisoner, like a bad mirror which tells us of nothing but itself." In Kleist's praise—and how un-German it sounds—of limpidity, his target was not philosophy in particular. Yet his is the best possible critique of philosophical jargon, a pseudo-language which, attempting to reflect ideas, merely assumes a contour at their expense, merely denatures and darkens them, merely calls attention to itself. By one of the most troublesome of all usurpations, the word has taken the leading role in a realm where it should be imperceptible.

§

"O Satan, my Master, I give myself unto thee forever!" How I regret not remembering the name of the nun who, having written these words with a nail dipped in her own blood, deserves to figure in an anthology of prayer and concision.

§

Consciousness is much more than the thorn, it is the *dagger* in the flesh.

§

Ferocity occurs in all conditions save in joy. *Schadenfreude*, malicious joy, is a misrepresentation. To do evil is a pleasure, not a joy. Joy, the one true victory over the world, is pure in its essence, hence irreducible to pleasure, which is always suspect, both in itself and in its manifestations.

§

An existence constantly transfigured by failure.

§

The wise man consents to everything, for he identifies himself with nothing. An opportunist *without desires*.

§

Nature's great mistake was to have been unable to confine herself to one "kingdom": juxtaposed with the vegetable, everything else seems inopportune, out of place. The sun should have sulked at the appearance of the first insect, and gone out altogether with the advent of the chimpanzee.

§

If, as we grow older, we scrutinize our own past at the expense of "problems," it is simply because we handle memories more readily than ideas.

§

The last whose disloyalty we forgive are those we have disappointed.

§

What other people do we always feel we could do better. Unfortunately we do not have the same feeling about what we ourselves do.

§

"I was the Prophet," Mohammed informs us, "when Adam was still between the water and the clay." . . . When we have not had the pride to found a religion—or at least to destroy one—how do we dare show ourselves in the light of day?

§

Detachment cannot be learned: it is inscribed in a civilization. We do not tend toward it, we discover it in ourselves. I was thinking this when I read that a missionary, after eighteen years in Japan, had made only sixty converts, and old ones at that. Moreover they escaped him at the last moment, dying in Japanese fashion, without remorse, without torments, worthy descendants of their ancestors who, to inure themselves, in the days of the Mongol wars, let themselves be impregnated by the nothingness of all things and by their own nothingness.

§

We can meditate upon eternity only in a prone position. For a considerable period, eternity was the Orientals' principal concern: did they not prefer the horizontal position? Once we lie down, time ceases to pass, to count. History is the product of a race that *stands*. As a vertical animal, man was to get into the habit of looking ahead, not only in space but in time as well. To which wretched origins we may trace the Future!

§

Every misanthrope, however sincere, at times reminds me of that old poet, bedridden and utterly forgotten, who in a rage with his contemporaries declared he would receive none of them. His wife, out of charity, would ring at the door from time to time. . . .

§

A work is finished when we can no longer improve it, though we know it to be inadequate and incomplete. We are so overtaxed by it that we no longer have the power to add a single comma, however indispensable. What determines the degree to which a work is done is not a requirement of art or of truth, it is exhaustion and, even more, disgust.

§

Whereas any sentence one has to write requires a pretense of invention, it takes little enough attention to enter into a text, even a difficult one. To scribble a postcard comes closer to creative activity than to read *The Phenomenology of Mind.*

§

Buddhism calls anger "corruption of the mind," manicheism "root of the tree of death." I know this, but what good does it do me to know?

§

She meant absolutely nothing to me. Realizing, suddenly, after so many years, that whatever happens I shall never see her again, I nearly collapsed. We understand what death is only by suddenly remembering the face of someone who has been a matter of indifference to us.

§

As art sinks into paralysis, artists multiply. This anomaly ceases to be one if we realize that art, on its way to exhaustion, has become both impossible and easy.

§

No one is responsible for what he is nor even for what he does. This is obvious and everyone more or less agrees that it is so. Then why celebrate or denigrate? Because to exist is to evaluate, to emit judgments, and because abstention, when it is not the effect of apathy or cowardice, requires an effort no one manages to make.

§

Every form of haste, even toward the good, betrays some mental disorder.

§

The least impure thoughts are those which appear between our anxieties, in the intervals of our annoyance, in those deluxe moments our misery grants itself.

§

Imaginary pains are by far the most real we suffer, since we feel a constant need for them and invent them because there is no way of doing without them.

§

If it is characteristic of the wise man to do nothing useless, no one will surpass me in wisdom: I do not even lower myself to useful things.

§

Impossible to imagine a degraded animal, a sub-animal.

§

O to have been born before man!

§

Try as I will, I cannot manage to scorn all those centuries during which men busied themselves with nothing more than perfecting a definition of God.

§

The most effective way to avoid dejection, motivated or gratuitous, is to take a dictionary, preferably of a language you scarcely know, and to look up word after word in it, making sure that they are the kind you will never use. . . .

§

As long as you live on this side of the terrible, you will find words to express it; once you know it from inside, you will no longer find a single one.

§

There is no limit-disappointment.

§

Grievances of every kind pass, but their source abides, and nothing has any effect on it: unassailable and unvarying, it is our *fatum*.

§

To realize, in rage and desolation alike, that nature, as Bossuet says, will not long grant us "this morsel of matter she lends."—*This morsel of matter:* by dint of pondering it we reach peace, though a peace it would be better never to have known.

§

Paradox is not suited to burials, nor to weddings or births, in fact. Sinister—or grotesque—events require commonplaces; the terrible, like the painful, accommodates only the cliché.

§

However disabused one may be, it is impossible to live without any hope at all. We always keep one, unwittingly, and this unconscious hope makes up for all the explicit others we have rejected, exhausted.

§

The more laden he is with years, the more readily he speaks of his death as a distant, quite unlikely event. Life is now such a habit that he has become unfit for death.

§

A blind man, authentically blind for once, held out his hand: in his posture, his rigidity, there was something that caught you, that made you hold your breath. He was handing you his blindness.

§

We forgive only madmen and children for being frank with us: others, if they have the audacity to imitate them, will regret it sooner or later.

§

To be "happy" you must constantly bear in mind the miseries you have escaped. This would be a way for memory to redeem itself, since ordinarily it preserves only disasters, eager—and with what success!—to sabotage happiness.

§

After a sleepless night, the people in the street seem automatons. No one seems to breathe, to walk. Each looks as if he is worked by clockwork: nothing spontaneous; mechanical smiles, spectral gesticulations. Yourself a specter, how would you see others as alive?

§

To be sterile—with so many sensations! Perpetual poetry without words.

§

Pure fatigue—fatigue without cause, the kind that comes like a gift or a scourge: that is what helps me pull myself together, that is what affords me knowledge of my "self." Once it leaves me, I am no more than an inanimate object.

§

Anything in folklore that remains alive comes from before Christianity. —The same is true of whatever is alive in each of us.

§

A man who fears ridicule will never go far, for good or ill: he remains on this side of his talents, and even if he has genius, he is doomed to mediocrity.

§

"Amid your most intense activities, pause a moment to 'consider' your mind"—this advice is surely not offered to those who "consider" their minds night and day, and who thereby have no need to suspend their activities, for the good reason that they engage in none.

§

Only what has been conceived in solitude, *face to face with God*, endures—whether one is a believer or not.

§

A passion for music is in itself an *avowal*. We know more about a stranger who yields himself up to it than about someone who is deaf to music and whom we see every day.

§

No meditation without a tendency to repetitiveness.

§

As long as God had him in tow, man advanced slowly, so slowly he did not even realize it. Now that he no longer lives in anyone's shadow, he is in a rush, and deplores it—he would give anything to regain the old cadence.

§

We have lost, being born, as much as we shall lose, dying. Everything.

§

Satiety—I have just now uttered this word, and already I no longer know apropos of what, so readily does it apply to everything I feel and think, to everything I love and loathe, to satiety itself.

§

I have killed no one, I have done better: I have killed the Possible, and like Macbeth, what I need most is to pray, but like him too, I cannot say *Amen*.

4

To deliver blows none of which land, to attack everyone without anyone's noticing, to shoot arrows whose poison you alone receive!

§

X, whom I have always treated as badly as I could, does not resent me because he resents no one. He forgives every insult, he even forgets them. How I envy him! To be like him, I should have to live through several existences and exhaust all my possibilities of transmigration.

§

In the days when I set off on month-long bicycle trips across France, my greatest pleasure was to stop in country cemeteries, to stretch out between two graves, and to smoke for hours on end. I think of those days as the most active period of my life.

§

How can you control yourself, master your behavior, when you come from a country where people howl at funerals?

§

On certain mornings, no sooner have I stepped out the door than I hear voices calling my name. Am I really me? Is it really my name? It is, it fills all space, it is on the lips of every passerby. Each pronounces it, even that woman in the next telephone booth, at the post office.

Sleepless nights devour the last vestiges of our common sense, our modesty, and would rob us of our reason, if the fear of ridicule didn't come to save us.

§

My curiosity and my repulsion, as well as my terror under his oily, metallic gaze, his obsequiousness, his unvarnished cunning, his strangely unveiled hypocrisy, his continual and obvious dissimulations, that mixture of scoundrel and madman . . . His insincerity is evident in each gesture, in every word. Insincerity isn't the right word, for to be insincere is to conceal the truth, and to know the truth, but in him there is no trace, no notion, no atom of truth, nor of lying either, nothing but a loathesome covetousness, a calculating lunacy. . . .

§

Around midnight, a woman in tears comes up to me in the street: "They've knifed my husband, France is disgusting, luckily I'm from Brittany, they took away my children, they kept me on drugs for six months. . . ." Not having realized at first that she was mad, so real her agony seemed (and in a sense was), I let her chatter on for a good half hour: talking did her good. Then I abandoned her, telling myself that the difference between us would be infinitesimal if I began to pour out my recriminations to the first comer.

§

A professor in an Eastern European country tells me that his mother, a peasant woman, was astonished to find out he was suffering from insomnia. When sleep didn't come, all *she* had to do was imagine a huge wheatfield swaying in the wind and she fell asleep at once.

With the image of a city, one would not arrive at the same result. It is inexplicable and miraculous that any city-dweller ever manages to close an eye.

§

The little tavern is frequented by the old men who live in the home at the end of the village. They come here, sitting with a glass in one hand, staring at each other without a word. One of them begins telling something he thinks is funny. No one listens, in any case no one laughs. All of them have drudged for years to get here. In the old days, in the countryside, someone would have smothered them under a pillow. A wise recipe, perfected by each family, and incomparably more humane than this one: gathering them together, sitting them here and curing them of boredom by stupor.

§

According to the Bible, it is Cain who created the first city, in order to have, as Bossuet puts it, a place *wherein to elude his remorse.* What a judgment! And how many times have I not felt its accuracy in my night walks through Paris!

§

One night, climbing the stairs in the dark, I was halted by an invincible force rising from both within and without. Unable to take another step, I stood there nailed to the spot, petrified. IMPOSSIBILITY—this ordinary word came, more apropos than usual, to enlighten me as to myself, no less than as to the word as well: it had so often come to my aid, yet never as now. At last I understood, definitively, what it meant. . . .

§

An ancient cleaning woman, in answer to my "How's everything going?" answers without looking up: "Taking its course." This ultra-banal answer nearly brings me to tears.

The more such turns of speech, which deal with becoming, with the passage of time, with the *course* of things, are worn down, the more likely they are to acquire the quality of a revelation. But the truth is not that they create an exceptional state, only that you yourself were in that state without realizing it, and that it required only a sign or a pretext for the extraordinary to occur.

§

We lived in the country, I went to school, and—an important detail—I slept in my parents' room. At night it was my father's habit to read aloud to my mother. Though he was a Greek Orthodox priest, he would read anything, doubtless assuming that at my age I wouldn't understand. Usually I didn't even listen and fell asleep, unless the text was some gripping story. One night I pricked up my ears. He was reading the scene from a biography of Rasputin where the father, on his deathbed, calls his son to him and says: "Go to Saint Petersburg and make yourself master of the city, fear nothing and no one, *for God is an old hog.*"

Such an enormity in my father's mouth, for whom the

priesthood was not a joke, impressed me as much as a conflagration or an earthquake. But I also distinctly recall—this was over fifty years ago—that my emotion was followed by a strange, dare I say a perverse pleasure.

§

Having penetrated, in the course of years, quite deeply into two or three religions, I have always retreated on the threshold of "conversion," lest I lie to myself. None of them was, in my eyes, free enough to admit that vengeance is a need, the most intense and profound of all, and that each man must satisfy it, if only in words. If we stifle that need, we expose ourselves to serious disturbances. More than one disorder—perhaps all disorders—derive from a vengeance too long postponed. We must learn how to explode! Any disease is *healthier* than the one provoked by a hoarded rage.

§

Philosophy in the Morgue. "My nephew was obviously a failure. If he had succeeded in making something of himself he would have had a different ending than . . . this." "You know, Madame," I replied to the monumental matron who had addressed me, "whether one succeeds or not comes down to the same thing." "You're right," she said, after a few seconds' thought. This unexpected acquiescence on the part of such a woman moved me almost as much as the death of my friend.

§

Misfits . . . It seems to me that their *adventure*, more than any other, sheds a light on the future, that they alone allow us to glimpse and to decipher it, and that if we set their exploits aside we utterly disqualify ourselves from *describing* the days to come.

§

"A pity," you were saying, "that N has never produced anything."

"So what! He exists. If he had given birth to books, if he had had the misfortune to 'realize' himself, we wouldn't have been talking about him the last hour." The advantage of being someone is rarer than that of creating. To produce is easy; what is difficult is to scorn the use of one's gifts.

§

Filming a scene, there are countless takes of the same incident. Someone watching in the street—obviously a provincial—can't get over it: "After this, I'll never go to the movies again."

One might react similarly with regard to anything whose *underside* one has seen, whose secret one has seized. Yet, by an obnubilation which has something of the miraculous about it, there are gynecologists who are attracted to their patients, gravediggers who father children, incurables who lay plans, skeptics who write. . . .

§

T, a rabbi's son, complains that this age of unprecedented persecutions has seen the birth of no *original* prayer capable of being adopted by the community and uttered in the synagogues. I assure him that he is mistaken to be distressed or alarmed by the fact: the great disasters yield nothing on the literary or religious level. Only the semi-misfortunes are fruitful, because they can be, because they are a point of departure, whereas too perfect a hell is almost as sterile as paradise.

§

I was twenty. Everything was a burden. One day I collapsed on a couch with an "I can't take it any longer." My mother, already driven distracted by my sleepless nights, told me she had just had a mass said for my "rest." *Not one but thirty thousand,* I would have liked to shout at her, thinking of the figure Charles V inscribed in his will—for a much longer rest, true enough.

§

I ran across him again, quite by chance, after twenty-five years. Unchanged, intact, fresher than ever, he actually seems to have retreated toward adolescence.

Where has he been hiding, and what has he done to escape the action of the years, to avoid our wrinkles and grimaces? And how has he lived, if in fact he has lived at all? Actually, a ghost. He must have cheated, he has not performed his duty as a living man, not played the game. A ghost, yes, and a gate-crasher. I discern no sign of destruction on his countenance, none of those marks which testify that one is a real being, an individual and not an apparition. What can I say to him? I feel awkward, embarrassed, even afraid. So greatly are we upset by anyone who escapes time, or merely deceives it.

§

D.C., who was writing his recollections of childhood in his Rumanian village, having told his neighbor, a peasant named Coman, that he wouldn't be left out, received a visit from the latter early the next day: "I know I'm a worthless man but all the same I didn't think I had fallen so low as to be talked about in a book."

How superior the oral world was to ours! Beings (I should say, peoples) live in the truth only as long as they have a horror of the written. Once they catch the virus, they enter the inauthentic, they lose their old superstitions to acquire a new one, worse than all the others combined.

§

Incapable of getting up, nailed to my bed, I drift with the whims of my memory, and I see myself wandering, as a child, in the Carpathians. One day I stumbled on a dog whose master, doubtless to be rid of it, had tied it to a tree; the animal was little more than a skeleton, so drained of life that it barely had the strength to look at me, without being able to move. Yet it was *standing*, that dog. . . .

§

A stranger comes and tells me he has killed someone. He is not wanted by the police because no one suspects him. I am the only one who knows he is the killer. What am I to do? I lack the courage as well as the treachery (for he has entrusted me with a secret—and what a secret!) to turn him in. I feel I am his accomplice, and resign myself to being arrested and punished as such. At the same time, I tell myself this would be too ridiculous. Perhaps I shall go and denounce him all the same. And so on, until I wake up.

The interminable is the specialty of the indecisive. They cannot mark life out for their own, and still less their dreams, in which they perpetuate their hesitations, pusillanimities, scruples. They are ideally qualified for nightmare.

§

A film about wild animals: endless cruelty in every latitude. "Nature," a torturer of genius, steeped in herself and her work, exults with good reason: there is not a moment when what is alive fails to tremble, to make others tremble. Pity is a strange luxury only the most perfidious and the fiercest creature could invent, out of a need to punish and torture itself—out of ferocity, still.

§

On a poster which, at a church door, announces *The Art of the Fugue*, someone has scrawled in huge letters: *God is dead.* This apropos of the composer who testifies that God, in the event of his decease, can revive precisely while we are listening to certain cantatas, certain fugues!

§

We have spent a little over an hour together. He has used the time to show off, and by dint of trying to say interesting things about himself, has succeeded. If he had merely swaggered in moderation, I should have found him a bore and left in a few minutes. By exaggerating, by playing the peacock to perfection, he has come close enough to wit to show some. The desire to appear subtle does not destroy subtlety. A mental defective, if he could feel the longing to astonish, would manage to deceive us—would even catch up with intelligence.

§

X, who is older than the patriarchs, after inveighing, during a long tête-à-tête, against this one and that, tells me: "The great weakness of my life is that I've never hated anyone." Our hatred does not diminish with the years: in fact, it mounts. That of an old man like X attains incredible proportions: now insensitive to his former affections, he puts all his faculties at the service of his rancors which, miraculously reinvigorated, will survive the crumbling of his memory and even of his reason.

. . . The danger of frequenting the old is that when we find them so far from detachment and so incapable of espousing it, we arrogate to ourselves all the advantages they are supposed to have and do not. And it is inevitable that our real or imaginary advance upon them in matters of weariness or disgust should incite to presumption.

§

Every family has its own philosophy. One of my cousins, who died young, once wrote me: "It's all the way it's always been and probably always will be until there's nothing left any more."

Whereas my mother ended the last note she ever sent me with this testamentary sentence: "Whatever people try to do, they'll regret it sooner or later."

Nor can I even boast of having acquired this vice of regret by my own setbacks. It precedes me, it participates in the patrimony of my tribe. What a legacy, such unfitness for illusion!

§

A few kilometers from the village where I was born, there was a hamlet, perched on a hill and inhabited solely by gypsies. In 1910 an amateur ethnologist visited the place, accompanied by a photographer. He managed to collect the inhabitants, who agreed to let their picture be taken, without knowing what that meant. At the instant they were asked to hold still, an old woman shrieked: "Watch out, they're stealing our souls!"

Whereupon they all flung themselves upon the two visitors, who had the greatest difficulty making their escape.

These half-savage gypsies—what were they but India, their land of origin which, under these circumstances, was speaking through them?

§

In continual rebellion against my ancestry, I have spent my whole life wanting to be something else: Spanish, Russian, cannibal—anything, except what I was. It is an aberration to want to be different from what you are, to espouse in theory any and every condition, except your own.

§

The day I read the list of nearly all the Sanskrit words that designate the absolute, I realized that I had taken the wrong path, the wrong country, the wrong idiom.

§

A friend, after I don't know how many years of silence, writes that she hasn't much longer to live, and that she is preparing to "enter the Unknown. . . ." The cliché gives me a start. I find it hard to see *what* one might enter by death. Any affirmation, in this realm, seems to me a delusion. Death is not a state, perhaps not even a transition. Then what is it? And by what cliché, in my turn, will I answer my friend?

§

I may change my opinion on the same subject, the same event, ten, twenty, thirty times in the course of a single day. And to think that each time, like the worst impostor, I dare utter the word "truth"!

Hale and hearty still, the woman dragged her husband after her, a tall, hunched man, eyes staring; she dragged him as if he had been the survivor of another age, an apoplectic and suppliant diplodocus.

An hour later, a second encounter: a neatly dressed old woman, extremely stooped, "advanced" toward me; her body forming a perfect half-circle, she necessarily kept her eyes on the ground, doubtless counting her unimaginable slow tiny foot-steps. It was as if she were learning how to walk, as if she were afraid of not knowing how and where to place her feet in order to move.

. . . Everything is good which brings me closer to Buddha.

§

Despite her white hair, she still paraded up and down her part of the sidewalk, looking for customers. I would run into her often, at three in the morning, and never felt like going home until I had heard her tell a few anecdotes or exploits. I have forgotten anecdotes and exploits alike, but not the readiness with which, one night when I had begun storming against all the sleeping "vermin" of Paris, she broke in with her forefinger pointing to heaven and: "What about the vermin *up there?*"

§

"Everything is without basis, without substance," and I never repeat it to myself without feeling something like happiness. Unfortunately there are so many moments when I fail to repeat it to myself.

5

I read him for the shipwrecked feeling I get from anything he writes. At first you follow, then you start going in circles, then you are caught up in a kind of mild unmenacing whirlpool, and you tell yourself you're sinking, and then you do sink. But you don't really drown—that would be too easy! You come back up to the surface, you follow all over again, amazed to see he seems to be saying something and to understand what it is, and then you start going round and round again, and you sink once more. . . . All of which is meant to be profound, and seems so. But once you come to your senses you realize it's only abstruse, obscure, and that the distance between real profundity and the willed kind is as great as between a revelation and a whim.

§

Anyone who gives himself up to writing believes—without realizing the fact—that his work will survive the years, the ages, time itself. . . . If he *felt*, while he was at work on it, that it was perishable, he would leave off where he was, he could never finish. Activity and credulity are correlative terms.

§

"Laughter ceased, and after laughter smiles." This apparently naïve remark by a biographer of Alexsandr Blok defines to perfection the program of any and every downfall.

§

No easy matter, to speak of God when one is neither a believer nor an atheist: and it is undoubtedly the drama we all share, theologians included—no longer capable of being either one or the other.

§

For a writer, progress toward detachment and deliverance is an unprecedented disaster. He, more than anyone else, needs his defects: if he triumphs over them, he is lost. He must be careful, then, not to improve, for if he succeeds, he will regret it bitterly.

§

We must beware of whatever insights we have into ourselves. Our self-knowledge annoys and paralyzes our daimon—this is where we should look for the reason Socrates wrote nothing.

§

What makes bad poets worse is that they read only poets (just as bad philosophers read only philosophers), whereas they would benefit much more from a book of botany or geology. We are enriched only by frequenting disciplines remote from our own. This is true, of course, only for realms where the ego is rampant.

§

Tertullian tells us that in order to be cured, epileptics would go "and greedily suck the blood of criminals slaughtered in the arena." If I were to heed my instinct, this would be the one type of medication, no matter what the disease, which I would adopt.

§

What right have we to be annoyed by someone who calls us a monster? The monster is unique by definition, and solitude, even the solitude of infamy, supposes something positive, a peculiar election, but undeniably an election.

§

Two enemies—the same man *divided.*

§

"Never judge a man without putting yourself in his place." This old proverb makes all judgment impossible, for we judge someone only because, in fact, we cannot put ourselves in his place.

§

If you love your independence, you must lend yourself, in order to protect it, to every turpitude; you must risk ignominy itself.

§

Nothing more abominable than the critic and, a fortiori, the philosopher in each of us: if I were a poet, I should behave like Dylan Thomas, who, when people would discuss his poems in his presence, would drop to the floor in a fit of convulsions.

§

Anyone who bestirs himself commits one injustice after the next, without a trace of remorse. Just bad humor. —Remorse is for those who do nothing, who cannot act. It replaces action for them, consoles them for their ineffectuality.

§

Most of our troubles come from our first impulses. The slightest enthusiasm costs more than a crime.

§

Since we remember clearly only our ordeals, it is ultimately the sick, the persecuted, the victims in every realm who will have lived to the best advantage. The others—the lucky ones—have a life, of course, but not the *memory* of a life.

§

What a bore, someone who doesn't deign to make an impression. Vain people are almost always annoying, but they make an effort, they take the trouble: they are bores who don't want to be bores, and we are grateful to them for that: we end by enduring them, even by seeking them out. On the other hand, we turn livid with fury in the presence of someone who pays no attention whatever to the effect he makes. What are we to say to him, and what are we to expect from him? Either keep some vestiges of the monkey, or else stay home.

§

Not the fear of effort but the fear of success explains more than one failure.

§

I'd like to pray with dagger-words. Unfortunately, if you pray at all, you have to pray like everyone else. Wherein abides one of the greatest difficulties of faith.

§

We dread the future only when we are not sure we can kill ourselves when we want to.

§

Neither Bossuet, nor Malebranche, nor Fénelon deigned to mention the *Pensées*: apparently Pascal didn't strike them as sufficiently *serious*.

§

Fear is the antidote to boredom: the remedy must be stronger than the disease.

§

If only I could reach the level of the man I would have liked to be! But some power, increasing year by year, draws me down. Even to get back up to *my* surface, I have to employ stratagems I cannot think of without blushing.

§

There was a time when, in order to dispel any impulse of vengeance once I had endured some affront, I would imagine myself quite still in my grave. And I calmed down at once. We must not despise our corpse too much: it can be useful on occasion.

§

Every thought derives from a thwarted sensation.

§

The only way to reach another person at any depth is to move toward what is deepest in yourself. In other words, to take the opposite path from the one followed by so-called generous minds.

§

If only I could say with that Hasidic rabbi: "The blessing of my life is that I have never needed a thing before I possessed it!"

§

In permitting man, Nature has committed much more than a mistake in her calculations: a crime against herself.

§

Fear creates *consciousness*—not natural fear but morbid fear. Otherwise animals would have achieved a level of consciousness higher than ours.

§

As orangutang in the strict sense of the word, man is old; as *historical* orangutang, he is comparatively recent: a parvenu who has not had time to learn how to behave in life.

§

After certain experiences, we should change names, since we ourselves are no longer the same. Everything assumes another aspect, starting with death. Which seems close and desirable: we are reconciled to it, and we reach the point of calling it "man's best friend," as Mozart does in a letter to his dying father.

§

We must suffer to the end, to the moment when we stop *believing* in suffering.

§

"Truth remains hidden to the man filled with desire and hatred" (Buddha). . . . Which is to say, to every man *alive.*

§

Won over by solitude, yet he remains in the world: a stylite *without a pillar.*

§

"You were wrong to count on me." Who can speak in such terms? God and the Failure.

§

Everything we achieve, everything that comes out of us, aspires to forget its origins, and succeeds only by opposing us. Hence the negative sign that marks all our successes.

§

There is nothing to say about anything. So there can be no limit to the number of books.

§

Failure, even repeated, always seems fresh; whereas success, multiplied, loses all interest, all attraction. It is not misfortune but happiness—insolent happiness, it is true—which leads to rancor and sarcasm.

§

"An enemy is as useful as a Buddha." Exactly, for our enemy watches over us, keeps us from letting ourselves go. By indicating, by divulging our least weakness, he leads us straight to our salvation, moves heaven and earth to keep us from being unworthy of his image of us. Hence our gratitude to him should be boundless.

§

We get a better hold of ourselves and of being when we have reacted against negating, dissolving books—against their noxious power. Fortifying books, actually, since they provoke the very energy which denies them. The more poison they contain, the more salutary their effect, provided we read them against the grain, as we should read any book, starting with the catechism.

§

The greatest favor we can do an author is to forbid him to work during a certain period. Short-term tyrannies are necessary—prohibitions which would suspend all intellectual activity. *Uninterrupted* freedom of expression exposes talent to a deadly danger, forces it beyond its means and keeps it from stockpiling sensations and experiences. Unlimited freedom is a crime against the mind.

§

Self-pity is not so sterile as we suppose. Once we feel its mere onset, we assume a thinker's attitude, and come to think of it, we come to think!

§

The stoic's maxim, according to which we should submit uncomplainingly to things which do not depend on ourselves, takes into account only external misfortunes, which escape our will. But how to accommodate ourselves to those which come from ourselves? If we are the source of our ills, whom are we to confront? Ourselves? We manage, luckily, to forget that we are the guilty parties, and moreover existence is tolerable only if we daily renew this lie, this act of oblivion.

§

All my life, I have lived with the feeling that I have been kept from my true place. If the expression "metaphysical exile" had no meaning, my existence alone would afford it one.

§

The more gifted a man is, the less progress he makes on the spiritual level. Talent is an obstacle to the inner life.

§

To save the word "grandeur" from officialdom, we should use it only apropos of insomnia or heresy.

§

In classical India, the sage and the saint were combined in one and the same person. To have any notion of such a success, we must imagine, if we can, a fusion between resignation and ecstasy, between a cold stoic and a disheveled mystic.

§

Being is suspect. Then what is to be said of "life," which is its deviation and stigma?

§

When someone tells us of an unfavorable opinion about ourselves, instead of being distressed, we should think of all the "evil" we have spoken of others, and realize that it is only justice that as much should be said of ourselves. Ironically, no one is more vulnerable, more susceptible, and less likely to acknowledge his own defects than the backbiter. Merely tell him about the slightest reservation someone has made in his regard, and he will lose countenance, lose his temper, and drown in his own bile.

§

Seen from the outside, harmony reigns in every sect, clan, and party; seen from the inside, discord. Conflicts in a monastery are as frequent and as envenomed as in any society. Even when they desert hell, men do so only to reconstruct it elsewhere.

§

The least conversion is experienced as an advance. Fortunately there exist exceptions.

One of my favorites is that eighteenth-century Jewish sect in which men went over to Christianity in order to debase themselves; and another is that South American Indian who, upon conversion, lamented that he must now become the prey of worms instead of being eaten by his children, an honor he would have enjoyed had he not abjured his tribe's beliefs.

§

Only normal that man should no longer be interested in religion but in religions, for only through them will he be in a position to understand the many versions of his spiritual collapse.

§

When we recapitulate the stages of our career, it is humiliating to realize that we have not had the disasters we deserved, the ones we were entitled to expect.

§

In some men, the prospect of a more or less imminent end excites energy, good or bad, and plunges them into a frenzy of activity. Artless enough to try to perpetuate themselves by their endeavor, by their work, they move heaven and earth to finish, to conclude it: not a moment to lose.

The same perspective invites others to founder in what's-the-use, in a stagnant clear-sightedness, in the unimpeachable truths of despond.

§

"My curse on the man who, in future editions of my works, knowingly changes anything—a sentence, or only a word, a syllable, a letter, a punctuation mark!" Is it the philosopher or the writer in Schopenhauer who speaks this way? Both at once, and this conjunction (when we think of the awful style of any philosophical work) is extremely rare. It is not a Hegel who would have uttered such a curse. Nor any other major philosopher, except Plato.

§

Nothing more aggravating than a seamless, unremitting irony which leaves you no time to breathe and still less to think; which instead of being inconspicuous, occasional, is massive, automatic, at the antipodes of its essentially delicate nature.

Which in any case is how it is used in Germany, a nation which, having meditated upon it the most, is least capable of wielding it.

§

Anxiety is not provoked: it tries to find a justification for itself, and in order to do so seizes upon anything, the vilest pretexts, to which it clings once it has invented them. A reality which precedes its particular expressions, its varieties, anxiety provokes itself, engenders itself, it is "infinite creation," and as such is more likely to suggest the workings of the divinity than those of the psyche.

§

Automatic melancholy: an elegiac robot.

§

At a grave, the words: game, imposture, joke, dream, come to mind. Impossible to think that existence is a serious phenomenon. Certainty of faking from the start, at bottom. Over the gate of our cemeteries should be written: "Nothing Is Tragic. Everything Is Unreal."

§

I shall not soon forget the expression of horror on what was his face, the dread, the extreme suffering, and the aggression. No, he was not happy. Never have I seen a man so uncomfortable in his coffin.

§

Look neither ahead nor behind, look into yourself, with neither fear nor regret. No one descends into himself so long as he remains a slave of the past or of the future.

§

Inelegant to reproach a man for his sterility, when that is his postulate, his mode of achievement, his dream. . . .

§

Nights when we have slept are as if they had never been. The only ones that remain in our memory are the ones when we couldn't close our eyes: *night* means sleepless night.

§

In order not to have to resolve them, I have turned all my practical difficulties into theoretical ones. Faced with the Insoluble, I breathe at last. . . .

§

To a student who wanted to know where I stood with regard to the author of *Zarathustra*, I replied that I had long since stopped reading him. Why? "I find him too *naïve*. . . ."

I hold his enthusiasms, his fervors against him. He demolished so many idols only to replace them with others: a false iconoclast, with adolescent aspects and a certain virginity, a certain innocence inherent in his solitary's career. He observed men only from a distance. Had he come closer, he could have neither conceived nor promulgated the superman, that preposterous, laughable, even grotesque chimera, a crotchet which could occur only to a mind without time to age, to know the long serene disgust of detachment.

Marcus Aurelius is much closer to me. Not a moment's hesitation between the lyricism of frenzy and the prose of acceptance: I find more comfort, more hope even, in the weary emperor than in the thundering prophet.

6

Appealing, that Hindu notion of entrusting our salvation to someone else, to a chosen "saint," and permitting him to pray in our place, to do anything in order to save us. Selling our soul to God. . . .

§

"Does talent have any need of passions? Yes, of many passions—repressed" (Joubert). Not one moralist we cannot convert into a precursor of Freud.

§

It is always surprising to discover that the great mystics produced so much, that they left so many treatises. Undoubtedly their intention was to celebrate God and nothing else. This is true in part, but only in part.

We do not create a body of work without attaching ourselves to it, without subjugating ourselves to it. Writing is the least ascetic of all actions.

§

When I lie awake far into the night, I am visited by my evil genius, as Brutus was by his before the battle of Philippi.

§

"Do I look like someone who has something to do here on earth?" —That's what I'd like to answer the busybodies who inquire into my activities.

§

It has been said that a metaphor "must be able to be drawn." Whatever is original and lasting in literature for at least a century contradicts this remark. For if anything has outlived its usefulness it is "coherent" metaphor, one with explicit contours. It is against such metaphor that poetry has unceasingly rebelled, to the point where a dead poetry is a poetry *afflicted* with coherence.

§

Listening to the weather report, I feel a strong response to the words "*scattered* rain." Which certainly proves that poetry is in ourselves and not in the expression, though *scattered* is an adjective capable of setting up a certain vibration.

§

Once I formulate a doubt, or more exactly, once I feel the need to formulate a doubt, I experience a curious, disturbing well-being. It would be far easier for me to live without a trace of belief than without a trace of doubt. Devasting doubt, nourishing doubt!

§

There is no *false* sensation.

§

Withdraw into yourself, perceive there a silence as old as being, even older. . . .

§

If I detest man, I could not say with the same ease: I detest the human *being*, for in spite of everything there is something more, something enigmatic and engaging in that word *being* which suggests qualities alien to the idea of man.

§

In the *Dhammapada*, it is suggested that, in order to achieve deliverance, we must be rid of the double yoke of Good and Evil. That Good itself should be one of our fetters we are too spiritually retarded to be able to admit. And so we shall not be delivered.

§

Everything turns on pain; the rest is accessory, even nonexistent, for we remember only what hurts. Painful sensations being the only real ones, it is virtually useless to experience others.

§

I believe with that madman Calvin that we are predestined to salvation or damnation in our mother's womb. We have already lived our life before being born.

§

A free man is one who has discerned the inanity of all points of view; a liberated man is one who has drawn the consequences of such discernment.

§

No sanctity without an inclination to scandal. This is true not only of saints; whoever *manifests* himself, in any way at all, proves he possesses a more or less developed taste for provocation.

§

I *feel* I am free but I *know* I am not.

§

I suppressed word after word from my vocabulary. When the massacre was over, only one had escaped: *Solitude.* I awakened euphoric.

§

If I have been able to hold out till now, it is because each blow, which seemed intolerable at the time, was followed by a second which was worse, then a third, and so on. If I were in hell, I'd want its circles to multiply, in order to count on a new ordeal, more trying than its predecessor. A salutary policy, with regard to torments at least.

§

What music appeals to in us it is difficult to know; what we do know is that music reaches a zone so deep that madness itself cannot penetrate there.

§

We should have been excused from lugging a body: the burden of the self was enough.

§

To recover a taste for certain things, to make my "soul" over, a nap of several cosmic epochs would be welcome.

§

I never could understand that friend who, back from Lapland, told me how oppressed he felt when for days on end he lived without seeing the slightest trace of mankind.

§

The flayed man as theoretician of detachment . . . The convulsionary as skeptic . . .

§

A burial in a Norman village. I ask for details from a farmer watching the procession from a distance. "*He* was still young, barely sixty. They found him dead in the field. Well, that's how it is. . . . That's how it is. . . ." This refrain, which struck me as comical at the time, has haunted me ever since. The fellow had no idea that what he was saying about death was all that can be said and all we know.

§

I like to read the way a chorus girl does: identifying myself with the author and the book. Any other attitude makes me think of dissecting corpses.

§

Whenever a man converts to something, anything, we envy him at first, then we pity him, after which we despise him.

§

We had nothing to say to one another, and while I was manufacturing my phrases I felt that the earth was falling through space and that I was falling with it at a speed that made me dizzy.

§

Years and years to waken from that sleep in which the others loll; then years and years to escape that awakening . . .

§

A task to be done, something I have undertaken out of necessity or choice: no sooner have I started in than everything seems important, everything attracts me, except *that*.

§

Think about those who haven't long to live, who know that everything is over and done with, except the time in which the thought of their end unrolls. Deal with that time. Write for *gladiators*. . . .

§

Erosion of our being by our infirmities: the resulting void is filled by the presence of consciousness, what am I saying?—that void *is* consciousness itself.

§

Moral disintegration when we spend time in a place that is too beautiful: the self dissolves upon contact with paradise. No doubt it was to avoid this danger that the first man made the choice he did.

§

All things considered, there have been more affirmations than negations—at least till now. So we may deny without remorse. Beliefs will always weigh more in the scales.

§

The substance of a work is the impossible—what we have not been able to attain, what could not be given to us: the sum of all the things which were refused us.

§

Gogol, in hopes of a "regeneration," journeys to Nazareth and discovers he is as bored there as "in a Russian railroad station"—this is what happens to us all when we look outside ourselves for what can exist only inside.

§

Kill yourself because you are what you are, yes, but not because all humanity would spit in your face!

§

Why fear the nothing in store for us when it is no different from the nothing which preceded us: this argument of the Ancients against the fear of death is unacceptable as consolation. *Before*, we had the luck not to exist; now we exist, and it is this particle of existence, hence of misfortune, which dreads death. Particle is not the word, since each of us prefers himself to the universe, at any rate considers himself equal to it.

§

When we discern the unreality of everything, we ourselves become unreal, we begin to survive ourselves, however powerful our vitality, however imperious our instincts. But they are no longer anything but false instincts, and false vitality.

§

If you are doomed to devour yourself, nothing can keep you from it: a trifle will impel you as much as a tragedy. Resign yourself to erosion at all times: your fate wills it so.

§

To live is to lose ground.

§

To think that so many have *succeeded* in dying!

§

Impossible not to resent those who write us overwhelming letters.

§

In a remote province of India, everything was explained by dreams, and what is more important, dreams were used to cure diseases as well. It was according to dreams that business was conducted and matters of life and death decided. Until the English came. Since then, one native said, "We no longer dream."

In what we have agreed to call "civilization," there resides, undeniably, a diabolic principle man has become conscious of too late, when it was no longer possible to remedy it.

§

Lucidity without the corrective of ambition leads to stagnation. It is essential that the one sustain the other, that the one combat the other *without winning*, for a work, for a life to be possible.

§

We cannot forgive those we have praised to the skies, we are impatient to break with them, to snap the most delicate chain of all: the chain of admiration . . . , not out of insolence, but out of an aspiration to find our bearings, to be free, to be . . . ourselves. Which we manage only by an act of injustice.

§

The problem of responsibility would have a meaning only if we had been consulted before our birth and had consented to be precisely who we are.

§

The energy and virulence of my *taedium vitae* continue to astound me. So much vigor in a disease so decrepit! To this paradox I owe my present incapacity to choose my final hour.

§

For our actions, for our vitality itself, the claim to lucidity is as ruinous as lucidity itself.

§

Children turn, and must turn, against their parents, and the parents can do nothing about it, for they are subject to a law which decrees the relations among all the living: i.e., that each engenders his own enemy.

§

So carefully have we been taught to cling to things that when we would be free of them, we do not know how to go about it. And if death did not come to our aid, our stubbornness in subsisting would make us find a recipe for existence beyond wearing out, beyond senility itself.

§

Everything is wonderfully clear if we admit that birth is a disastrous or at least an inopportune event; but if we think otherwise, we must resign ourselves to the unintelligible, or else cheat like everyone else.

§

In a Gnostic work of the second century of our era, we read: "The prayer of a melancholy man will never have the strength to rise unto God." . . . Since man prays only in despondency, we may deduce that no prayer has ever reached its destination.

§

He was above all others, and had had nothing to do with it: he had simply *forgotten* to desire. . . .

§

In ancient China, women suffering from anger or grief would climb onto platforms specially constructed for them in the street, and there would give free rein to their fury or their lamentations. Such confessionals should be revived and adopted the world over, if only to replace the obsolete ones of the Church, or the ineffectual ones of various therapeutics.

§

This philosopher lacks *keeping* or, to use the jargon, "internal form." He is too fabricated to be alive or even "real"—a sinister puppet. What bliss to know I shall never open his books again!

§

No one exclaims he is feeling well and that he is free, yet this is what all who know this double blessing should do. Nothing condemns us more than our incapacity to shout our good luck.

§

To have failed in everything, always, out of a love of discouragement!

§

The sole means of protecting your solitude is to offend everyone, beginning with those you love.

§

A book is a postponed suicide.

§

Say what we will, death is the best thing nature has found to please everyone. With each of us, everything vanishes, everything stops forever. What an advantage, what an abuse! Without the least effort on our part, we own the universe, we drag it into our own disappearance. No doubt about it, dying is immoral. . . .

7

If instead of expanding you, putting you in a state of energetic euphoria, your ordeals depress and embitter you, you can be sure you have no spiritual vocation.

§

To live in expectation, to count on the future or on a simulacrum of the future: we are so accustomed to it that we have conceived the idea of immortality only out of a need *to wait out eternity.*

§

Every friendship is an inconspicuous drama, a series of subtle wounds.

§

Luther Dead by Lucas Fortnagel. A plebeian, aggressive, terrifying mask, as of some sublime hog . . . which perfectly renders the features of the man we cannot sufficiently praise for having declared: "Dreams are liars; if you shit in your bed, that's true."

§

The more you live, the less useful it seems to have lived.

§

At twenty, those nights when for hours at a time I would stand, forehead pressed against the pane, staring into the dark. . . .

§

No autocrat wields a power comparable to that enjoyed by a poor devil planning to kill himself.

§

Educating yourself not to leave traces is a moment-by-moment war against yourself, solely to prove that you could, if you chose, become a sage. . . .

§

To exist is a state as little conceivable as its contrary. No, still more inconceivable.

§

In Antiquity, "books" were so costly that one could not accumulate them unless one was a king, a tyrant, or . . . Aristotle, the first to possess a library worthy of the name.

One more incriminating item in the dossier of a philosopher already so catastrophic in so many regards.

§

If I were to conform to my most intimate convictions, I should cease to take any action whatever, to react in any way. But I am still capable of *sensations*. . . .

§

A monster, however horrible, secretly attracts us, pursues us, haunts us. He represents, enlarged, our advantages and our miseries, he proclaims *us*, he is our standard-bearer.

§

Over the centuries, man has slaved to believe, passing from dogma to dogma, illusion to illusion, and has given very little time to doubts, short intervals between his epochs of blindness. Indeed they were not doubts but pauses, moments of respite following the fatigue of faith, of any faith.

§

Innocence being the perfect state, perhaps the only one, it is incomprehensible that a man enjoying it should seek to leave it. Yet history from its beginnings down to ourselves is only that and nothing but that.

§

I draw the curtains, and I wait. Actually, I am not waiting for anything, I am merely making myself *absent*. Scoured, if only for a few minutes, of the impurities which dim and clog the mind, I accede to a state of consciousness from which the self is evacuated, and I am as soothed as if I were resting outside the universe.

§

In one medieval exorcism, all the parts of the body, even the smallest, are listed from which the demon is ordered to depart: a kind of lunatic anatomy treatise, fascinating for its hypertrophy of precision, its profusion of unexpected details. A scrupulous incantation. *Leave the nails!* Fanatic but not without poetic effect. For authentic poetry has nothing in common with "poetry."

§

In all our dreams, even if they deal with the Flood, there is always, if only for a fraction of a second, some minuscule incident we witnessed the day before. This regularity, which I have verified for years, is the only constant, the only law or semblance of law I have been able to discern in night's incredible chaos.

§

The dissolving power of conversation. One realizes why both meditation and action require silence.

§

The certainty of being only an accident has accompanied me on all occasions, propitious or injurious, and if it has saved me from the temptation to believe myself necessary, it has not on the other hand entirely cured me of a certain vainglory inherent in the loss of illusions.

§

Rare to come upon a free mind, and when you do, you realize that the best of such a mind is not revealed in its works (when we write we bear, mysteriously, chains) but in those confidences where, released from conviction and pose, as from all concern with rigor or standing, it displays its weaknesses. And where it behaves as a heretic to itself.

§

If the foreigner is not a creator in the matter of language, it is because he wants to do *as well* as the natives: whether or not he succeeds, this ambition is his downfall.

§

I begin a letter over and over again, I get nowhere: what to say and how to say it? I don't even remember whom I was writing to. Only passion or profit find at once the right tone. Unfortunately detachment is indifference to language, insensitivity to words. Yet it is by losing contact with words that we lose contact with human beings.

§

Everyone has had, at a given moment, an extraordinary experience which will be for him, because of the memory of it he preserves, the crucial obstacle to his inner metamorphosis.

§

I know peace only when my ambitions sleep. Once they waken, anxiety repossesses me. Life is a state of ambition. The mole digging his tunnels is ambitious. Ambition is in effect everywhere, and we see its traces on the faces of the dead themselves.

§

Going to India because of the Vedanta or Buddhism is about the same as going to France because of Jansenism. Moreover the latter is more recent, since it vanished only three centuries ago.

§

Not the slightest trace of reality anywhere—except in my sensations of unreality.

§

Existence would be a quite impracticable enterprise if we stopped granting importance to what has none.

§

Why does the Gita rank "renunciation of the fruit of actions" so high? Because such renunciation is rare, impracticable, contrary to our nature, and because achieving it is destroying the man one has been and one is, killing in oneself the entire past, the work of millennia—in a word, freeing oneself of the Species, that hideous and immemorial riffraff.

§

We should have abided by our larval condition, dispensed with evolution, remained incomplete, delighting in the elemental siesta and calmly consuming ourselves in an embryonic ecstasy.

§

Truth abides in the individual drama. If I suffer authentically, I suffer much more than an individual, I transcend the sphere of my selfhood, I rejoin the essence of others. The only way to proceed toward the universal is to concern ourselves exclusively with what concerns ourselves.

§

When we are *fixated* on doubt, we take more pleasure in lavishing speculations upon it than in practicing it.

§

If you want to know a nation, frequent its second-order writers: they alone reflect its true nature. The others denounce or transfigure the nullity of their compatriots, and neither can nor will put themselves on the same level. They are suspect witnesses.

§

In my youth there would be weeks during which I never closed my eyes. I lived in the unlived world, I had the sense that Time, with all its moments, had concentrated itself within me, where it culminated, where it triumphed. I moved it onward, of course, I was its promoter and bearer, its cause and substance, and it was as an agent and accomplice that I participated in its apotheosis. When sleep departs from us, the unheard-of becomes everyday, easy: we enter it without preparations, inhabit it, wallow in it.

§

Astounding, the number of hours I have wasted on the "meaning" of what exists, of what happens. . . . But that "what" has no meaning, as all serious minds know. Hence they devote their time and their energy to more useful undertakings.

§

My affinities with Russian Byronism, from Pechorin to Stavrogin, my boredom and my passion for boredom.

§

X, whom I do not particularly appreciate, was telling a story so stupid that I wakened with a start: those we don't like rarely shine in our dreams.

§

For lack of occupation, the old seem to be trying to solve something very complicated, devoting to it all the capacities they still possess. Perhaps this is why they do not commit suicide en masse, as they ought were they even a trifle less absorbed.

§

Love at its most impassioned does not bring two human beings so close together as calumny. Inseparable, slanderer and slandered constitute a "transcendent" unity, forever welded one to the other. Nothing can separate them. One inflicts harm, the other endures it, but if he endures it, it is because he is accustomed to doing so, can no longer do without it, even insists upon it. He knows that his wishes will be gratified, that he will never be forgotten, that whatever happens he will be eternally present in the mind of his indefatigable benefactor.

§

The monk-errant, the wandering friar—so far, the supreme achievement. To reach the point of no longer having anything to renounce! Such must be the dream of any disabused mind.

§

Sobbing negation—the only tolerable form of negation.

§

Lucky Job, who was not obliged to annotate his lamentations!

§

Late at night. I feel like falling into a frenzy, doing some unprecedented thing to release myself, but I don't see against whom, against what. . . .

§

Mme d'Heudicourt, Saint-Simon observes, had never spoken good of anyone in her life without adding some crushing "but's."

A wonderful definition, not of backbiting but of conversation in general.

§

Everything that lives makes *noise*. What an argument for the mineral kingdom!

§

Bach was quarrelsome, litigious, self-serving, greedy for titles and honors, etc. So what! A musicologist listing the cantatas whose theme is death has remarked that no mortal ever had such a nostalgia for it. Which is all that counts. The rest has to do with biography.

§

The misfortune of being incapable of neutral states except by reflection and effort. What an idiot achieves at the outset, we must struggle night and day to attain, and only by fits and starts!

§

I have always lived with the vision of a host of moments marching against me. Time will have been my Birnam Wood.

§

Painful or wounding questions asked by the uncouth distress and anger us, and may have the same effect as certain techniques of Oriental meditation. Who knows if a dense, aggressive stupidity might not provoke illumination? It is certainly worth as much as a rap on the head with a stick.

§

Knowledge is not possible, and even if it were, would solve nothing. Such is the doubter's position. What does he want, then—what is he looking for? Neither he nor anyone will ever know. Skepticism is the rapture of impasse.

§

Besieged by others, I try to make my escape, without much success, it must be confessed. Yet I manage to wangle myself, day by day, a few seconds' audience with *the man I would have liked to be.*

§

By a certain age, we should change names and hide out somewhere, lost to the world, in no danger of seeing friends or enemies again, leading the peaceful life of an overworked malefactor.

§

We cannot reflect and be modest. Once the mind is set to work, it replaces God and anything else. It is indiscretion, encroachment, profanation. It does not build, it dislocates. The tension its methods betray reveals its brutal, implacable character: without a good dose of ferocity, we could not follow a thought to its conclusion.

§

Most subverters, visionaries, and saviors have been either epileptics or dyspeptics. There is unanimity as to the virtues of epilepsy; gastric upheavals are regarded, on the other hand, as less meritorious. Yet nothing is more conducive to subversion than a digestion which refuses to be forgotten.

§

My mission is to suffer for all those who suffer *without knowing it.* I must pay for them, expiate their unconsciousness, their luck to be ignorant of how unhappy they are.

§

Each time Time torments me, I tell myself that one of us must back down, that it is impossible for this cruel confrontation to go on indefinitely.

§

When we are in the depths of depression, everything which feeds it, affords it further substance, also raises it to a level where we can no longer follow and thereby renders it too great, excessive: scarcely surprising that we should reach the point of no longer regarding it as our own.

§

A foretold misfortune, when at last it occurs, is ten, is a hundred times harder to endure than one we did not expect. All during our apprehensions, we lived through it in advance, and when it happens these past torments are added to the present ones, and together they form a mass whose weight is intolerable.

§

Obviously God was a solution, and obviously none so satisfactory will ever be found again.

§

I shall never utterly admire anyone except a man dishonored—

and happy. There is a man, I should say, who defies the opinion of his fellows and who finds consolation and happiness in himself alone.

§

The man of the Rubicon, after Pharsalus, had forgiven too many. Such magnanimity seemed offensive to those of his friends who had betrayed him and whom he had humiliated by treating them without rancor. They felt diminished, flouted, and punished him for his clemency or for his disdain: he had refused to stoop to resentment! Had he behaved as a tyrant, they would have spared him. But they could not forgive him, since he had not deigned to frighten them enough.

§

Everything that *is* engenders, sooner or later, nightmares. Let us try, therefore, to invent something better than being.

§

Philosophy, which had made it its business to undermine beliefs, when it saw Christianity spreading and on the point of prevailing, made common cause with paganism, whose superstitions seemed preferable to the triumphant insanities. By attacking and demolishing the gods, philosophy had intended to free men's minds; in reality, it handed them over to a new servitude, worse than the old one, for the god who was to replace the gods had no particular weakness for either tolerance or irony.

Philosophy, it will be objected, is not responsible for the advent of this god, indeed this was not the god philosophy recommended. No doubt, but it should have suspected that we do not subvert the gods with impunity, that others would come to take their place, and that it had nothing to gain by the exchange.

§

Fanaticism is the death of conversation. We do not gossip with a candidate for martyrdom. What are we to say to someone who refuses to penetrate our reasons and who, the moment we do not bow to his, would rather die than yield? Give us dilettantes and sophists, who at least espouse *all* reasons. . . .

§

We invest ourselves with an abusive superiority when we tell someone what we think of him and of what he does. Frankness is not compatible with a delicate sentiment, nor even with an ethical exigency.

§

More than all others, our relatives are ready to doubt our merits. It is a universal rule: Buddha himself did not escape it—one of his cousins opposed him the most, and only afterward Mara, the devil.

§

For the victim of anxiety, there is no difference between success and fiasco. His reaction to the one is the same as to the other: both trouble him equally.

§

When I torment myself a little too much for not working, I tell myself that I might just as well be dead and that then I would be working still less. . . .

§

Rather in a gutter than on a pedestal.

§

The advantages of a state of eternal potentiality seem to me so considerable that when I begin listing them, I can't get over the fact that the transition to Being could ever have occurred.

§

Existence = Torment. The equation seems obvious to me, but not to one of my friends. How to convince him? I cannot *lend* him my sensations; yet only they would have the power to persuade him, to give him that additional dose of *ill-being* he has so insistently asked for all this time.

§

If we see things black, it is because we weigh them in the dark, because thoughts are generally the fruit of sleeplessness, consequently of darkness. They cannot adapt to life because they have not been thought *with a view* to life. The notion of the consequences they might involve doesn't even occur to the mind. We are beyond all human calculation, beyond any notion of salvation or perdition, of being or non-being, we are in a particular silence, a superior modality of the void.

§

Not yet to have digested the affront of being born.

§

To expend oneself in conversations as much as an epileptic in his fits.

§

In order to conquer panic or some tenacious anxiety, there is nothing like imagining your own burial. An effective method, readily available to all. In order not to have to resort to it too often in the course of a day, best to experience its benefit straight off, when you get up. Or else use it only at exceptional moments, like Pope Innocent IX, who, having commissioned a painting in which he was shown on his deathbed, glanced at it each time he had to make some important decision.

§

There is no negator who is not famished for some catastrophic *yes*.

§

We may be sure that man will never reach depths comparable to those he knew during the ages of egoistic colloquy with *his* God.

§

Not one moment when I am not external to the universe! . . . No sooner have I lamented over myself, pitying my wretched condition, than I realize that the terms in which I described my misfortune were precisely those which define the first characteristic of the "supreme being."

§

Aristotle, Aquinas, Hegel—three enslavers of the mind. The worst form of despotism is the *system*, in philosophy and in everything.

§

God is what survives the evidence that nothing deserves to be thought.

§

When I was young, no pleasure compared with the pleasure of making enemies. Now, whenever I make one, my first thought is to be reconciled, so that I won't have to bother about him. Having enemies is a heavy responsibility. My burden is sufficient, I no longer can carry that of others as well.

§

Joy is a light which devours itself, inexhaustibly; it is the sun *early on.*

§

A few days before he died, Claudel remarked that we should not call God infinite but inexhaustible. As if it did not come down to the same thing, or just about! All the same, this concern for exactitude, this verbal scruple at the moment that he was writing that his "lease" on life had nearly expired, is more inspiring than a "sublime" word or gesture.

§

The unusual is not a criterion. Paganini is more surprising and more unpredictable than Bach.

§

We should repeat to ourselves, every day: I am one of the billions dragging himself across the earth's surface. One, and no more. This banality justifies any conclusion, any behavior or action: debauchery, chastity, suicide, work, crime, sloth, or

rebellion. . . . Whence it follows that each man is right to do
what he does.

§

Tsimtsum. This silly-sounding word designates a major concept
of the Cabbala. For the world to exist, God, who was everything
and everywhere, consented to shrink, to leave a vacant space not
inhabited by Himself: it is in this "hole" that the world
occurred.

Thus we occupy the wasteland He conceded to us out of pity
or whim. For us to exist, He contracted, He limited His
sovereignty. We are the product of His voluntary reduction, of
His effacement, of His partial absence. In His madness He has
actually amputated Himself for us. If only He had had the good
sense and the good taste to remain *whole*!

§

In the "Gospel According to the Egyptians," Jesus proclaims:
"Men will be the victims of death so long as women give birth."
And he specifies: "I am come to destroy the works of woman."

When we frequent the extreme truths of the Gnostics, we
should like to go, if possible, still further, to say something never
said, which petrifies or pulverizes history, something out of a
cosmic Neronianism, out of a madness on the scale of matter.

§

To express an obsession is to project it outside yourself, to hunt
it down, to exorcise it. Obsessions are the *demons* of a world
without faith.

§

Man accepts death but not the hour of his death. To die any time, except when one has to die!

§

Once we step into a cemetery, a feeling of utter mockery does away with any metaphysical concern. Those who look for "mystery" everywhere do not necessarily get to the bottom of things. Most often "mystery," like "the absolute," corresponds only to a mannerism of the mind. It is a word we should use only when we cannot do otherwise, in really desperate cases.

§

If I recapitulate my plans which have remained plans and those which have worked out, I have every reason to regret that these latter have not suffered the fate of the former.

§

"He who is inclined to lust is merciful and tender-hearted; those who are inclined to purity are not so" (Saint John Climacus). It took a saint, neither more nor less, to denounce so distinctly and so vigorously not the lies but the very essence of Christian morality, and indeed of all morality.

§

We are not afraid to accept the notion of an uninterrupted sleep; on the other hand an eternal *awakening* (immortality, if it were conceivable, would be just that) plunges us into dread. Unconsciousness is a country, a fatherland; consciousness, an exile.

§

Any profound impression is voluptuous or funereal—or both at once.

§

No one has been so convinced as I of the futility of everything; and no one has taken so tragically so many futile things.

§

Ishi, the last American Indian of his tribe, after hiding for years in terror of the White Men, reduced to starvation, surrendered of his own free will to the exterminators of his people, believing that the same treatment was in store for himself. He was made much of. He had no posterity, he was truly the last.

Once humanity is destroyed or simply extinguished, we may imagine a sole survivor who would wander the earth, without even having anyone to surrender *to*. . . .

§

Deep in his heart, man aspires to rejoin the condition he had *before* consciousness. History is merely the detour he takes to get there.

§

Only one thing matters: learning to be the loser.

§

Every phenomenon is a corrupt version of another, larger phenomenon: time, a disease of eternity; history, a disease of time; life, again, a disease of matter.

Then what is normal, what is healthy? Eternity? Which itself is only an infirmity of God.

8

Without the notion of a failed universe, the spectacle of injustice in every system would put even an abulic into a straitjacket.

§

Annihilating affords a sense of power, flatters something obscure, something *original* in us. It is not by erecting but by pulverizing that we may divine the secret satisfactions of a god. Whence the lure of destruction and the illusions it provokes among the frenzied of any era.

§

Each generation lives in the absolute: it behaves as if it had reached the apex if not the end of history.

§

Any and every nation, at a certain moment of its career, considers itself *chosen*. It is at this moment that it gives the best and the worst of itself.

§

No accident that the Trappist order was founded in France rather than in Italy or Spain. Granted the Spanish and the Italians talk ceaselessly, but they do not *hear themselves* talk, whereas the Frenchman relishes his eloquence, never forgets he is talking, is consummately conscious of the fact. He alone could regard silence as an ordeal, as an *askesis*.

§

What spoils the French Revolution for me is that it all happens on stage, that its promoters are born actors, that the guillotine is merely a decor. The history of France, as a whole, seems a bespoke history, an *acted* history: everything in it is perfect from the theatrical point of view. It is a performance, a series of gestures and events which are watched rather than suffered, a spectacle that takes ten centuries to put on. Whence the impression of frivolity which even the Terror affords, seen from a distance.

§

Prosperous societies are far more fragile than the others, since it remains for them to achieve only their own ruin, comfort not being an ideal when we possess it, still less of one when it has been around for generations. Not to mention the fact that nature has not included well-being in her calculations and could not do so without perishing herself.

§

If all peoples turned apathetic at once, there would be no more conflicts, no more wars, no more empires. But unfortunately there are young peoples, and indeed young people—a major obstacle to the philanthropists' dreams: to bring it about that all men might reach the same degree of lassitude or ineffectuality. . . .

§

We must side with the oppressed on every occasion, even when they are in the wrong, though without losing sight of the fact that they are molded of the same clay as their oppressors.

§

Characteristic of dying regimes: to permit a confused mixture of beliefs and doctrines, and to give the illusion, at the same time, that the moment of choice can be indefinitely postponed . . .

This is the source—the sole source—of the charm of pre-revolutionary periods.

§

Only false values prevail, because everyone can assimilate them, counterfeit them (false thereby to the second degree). An idea that succeeds is necessarily a pseudo-idea.

§

Revolutions are the *sublime* of bad literature.

§

The unfortunate thing about public misfortunes is that everyone regards himself as qualified to talk about them.

§

The right to suppress everyone that bothers us should rank first in the constitution of the ideal State.

§

The only thing the young should be taught is that there is virtually nothing to be hoped for from life. One dreams of a *Catalogue of Disappointments* which would include all the disillusionments reserved for each and every one of us, to be posted in the schools.

§

According to the Princess Palatine, Mme de Maintenon was in the habit of repeating, during the years after the king's death when she had no further role to play: "For some time now, there has prevailed a spirit of vertigo which is spreading everywhere." This "spirit of vertigo" is what the losers have always noticed, correctly moreover, and we might well reconsider all history from the perspective of this formula.

§

Progress is the injustice each generation commits with regard to its predecessor.

§

The surfeited hate themselves—not secretly but publicly, and long to be swept away, one way or another. They prefer, in any case, that the sweeping be accomplished with their own cooperation. This is the most curious, the most original aspect of a revolutionary situation.

§

A nation generates only one revolution. The Germans have never repeated the exploit of the Reformation, or rather, they have repeated but not equaled it. France has remained an eternal tributary of '89. Equally true of Russia and of all nations, this tendency to plagiarize oneself in regard to revolutions is at once reassuring and distressing.

§

Romans of the decadence enjoyed only what they called Greek leisure *(otium graecum)*, the thing they had most despised in the period of their vigor. The analogy with today's civilizations is so flagrant it would be indecent to insist on it.

§

Alaric claimed that a "demon" drove him against Rome. Every exhausted civilization awaits its barbarian, and every barbarian awaits his demon.

§

The West: a sweet-smelling rottenness, a perfumed corpse.

§

All these nations were great because they had great prejudices. They now have none. Are they nations still? At most, disintegrated crowds.

§

The white race increasingly deserves the name given by the American Indians: *palefaces*.

§

In Europe, happiness stops at Vienna. Beyond, misery upon misery, since the beginning.

§

The Romans, the Turks, and the British could found lasting empires because, refractory to all doctrine, they imposed none upon the subject nations. They would never have managed to wield so long a hegemony had they been afflicted with some messianic vice. Unhoped-for oppressors, administrators, and parasites, lords without convictions, they had the art of combining authority and indifference, rigor and abandon. It is this art, the secret of the true master, which the Spaniards of old lacked, as it is lacking in the conquerors of our own day.

§

So long as a nation keeps the awareness of its superiority, it is fierce and respected; once it loses that awareness, a nation becomes humanized, and no longer counts.

§

When I rage against the age, I can calm myself merely by thinking of what will happen, of the retrospective jealousy of those who come after us. In certain respects, we belong to the old humanity, the humanity that could still regret paradise. But those who come after us will not even have the recourse of that regret, they will not even have an idea of it, not even the word!

§

My vision of the future is so *exact* that if I had children, I should strangle them here and now.

§

When we think of the Berlin salons in the Romantic period, of the role played in them by a Henrietta Herz or a Rachel Levin, of the friendship between the latter and Crown Prince Louis-Ferdinand; and when we then think that if such women had lived in this century they would have died in some gas chamber, we cannot help considering the belief in progress as the falsest and stupidest of superstitions.

§

Hesiod was the first to elaborate a philosophy of history. And also launched the notion of decadence. By doing so, what a light he casts on historical process! If, at the very outset, in the heart of the post-Homeric world, he decided that humanity was in its iron age, what would he have said a few centuries later—what would he say today?

Except in periods clouded over by frivolity or utopia, man has always believed himself on the threshold of the worst. Knowing what he knew, by what miracle could he have unceasingly varied his desires and his terrors?

§

When, just after the First World War, electricity was installed in the village where I was born, there was a general murmur of protest, then mute desolation. But when electricity was installed in the churches (there were three), everyone was convinced the Antichrist had come and, with him, the end of time.

These Carpathian peasants had seen clearly, had seen *far:* Emerging from prehistory, they knew already, in that day and age, what "civilized" men have known only recently.

§

It is my prejudice against everything that turns out well that has given me a taste for reading history.

Ideas are unsuited to a final agony; they die, of course, but without knowing how to die, whereas an event exists only with a view to its end. A sufficient reason to prefer the company of historians to that of philosophers.

§

During his famous embassy to Rome in the second century B.C., Carneades took advantage of the occasion to speak the first day in favor of the idea of justice, and on the following day against it. From that moment, philosophy, hitherto nonexistent in that country of healthy conduct, began to perpetrate its ravages. What is philosophy, then? *The worm in the fruit.* . . .

Cato the Censor, who had been present at the Greek's dialectical performances, was alarmed by them and asked the Senate to satisfy the Athenian delegation as soon as possible, so harmful and even dangerous did he consider their presence. Roman youth was not to frequent minds so destructive.

On the moral level, Carneades and his companions were as formidable as the Carthaginians on the military. Rising nations fear above all the absence of prejudices and prohibitions, the intellectual shamelessness which constitutes the allure of declining civilizations.

§

Hercules was punished for having succeeded in all his undertakings. Similarly Troy, too happy, had to perish.

Pondering this vision shared by the tragic poets, we cannot help thinking that the so-called free world, upon which every fortune has been lavished, will inevitably suffer Ilion's fate, for the jealousy of the gods survives their disappearance.

§

"The French don't want to work any more, they all want to *write,*" my concierge told me, unaware that she was then and there passing judgment on all old civilizations.

§

A society is doomed when it no longer has the force to be limited. How, with an open mind—too open—can it protect itself against the excesses, the mortal risks of freedom?

§

Ideological disputes reach the point of paroxysm only in countries where men have fought each other over words, where they have gone to death for words . . . , in the countries, in short, which have known wars of religion.

§

A nation which has exhausted its mission is like an author who repeats himself—no, who has nothing left to say. For to repeat yourself is to prove that you still believe in yourself, and in what you have said. But a declining nation no longer has even the strength to mouth its old mottoes, which once had assured it its preeminence and its pride.

§

French has become a provincial language. The natives don't mind. Only the foreigner is inconsolable on its account—he alone goes into mourning for Nuance. . . .

§

Themistocles, by a unanimously approved decree, had the interpreter of Xerxes' ambassadors put to death "for having dared use the Greek language to express the orders of a barbarian."

A people commits such an act only at the peak of its career. It is decadent, it is dying, when it no longer believes in its language, when it stops believing that its language is the supreme form of expression, *the* language.

§

A nineteenth-century philosopher maintained, in his innocence, that La Rochefoucauld was right *for the past,* but that he would be invalidated by the future. The idea of progress dishonors the intellect.

§

The further man proceeds, the less he is in a position to solve his problems, and when, at the apex of his blindness, he will be convinced he is on the point of success, then the unheard-of will occur.

§

I would bestir myself, at best, for the Apocalypse, but for a revolution . . . To collaborate with an ending or a genesis, an ultimate or initial calamity, yes, but not with a change for some better or worse. . . .

§

We have convictions only if we have studied nothing thoroughly.

§

In the long run, tolerance breeds more ills than intolerance. If this is true, it constitutes the most serious accusation that can be made against man.

§

Once the animals no longer need to fear each other, they fall into a daze and take on that dumbfounded look they have in zoos. Individuals and nations would afford the same spectacle if some day they managed to live in harmony, no longer trembling openly or in secret.

§

With sufficient perspective, nothing is good or bad. The historian who ventures to judge the past is writing journalism *in another century*.

§

In two hundred years (let us be precise!), the survivors of the overly fortunate nations will be put on reservations and visited, contemplated with disgust, commiseration, or stupor, and with a malicious admiration as well.

§

Monkeys living in groups reject, apparently, those which in some fashion have consorted with humans. How one regrets that Swift never knew such a detail!

§

Are we to execrate our age—or all ages?
Do we think of Buddha withdrawing from the world *on account of his contemporaries*?

§

If humanity has such love for saviors, those fanatics who so shamelessly believe in themselves, it is because humanity supposes they believe in it.

§

The strength of this Statesman is to be visionary and cynical. A dreamer *without scruples*.

§

The worst crimes are committed out of enthusiasm, a morbid state responsible for almost all public and private disasters.

§

The future appeals to you? All yours! Myself I prefer to keep to the incredible present and the incredible past. I leave it to you to face the Incredible itself.

§

"You're against everything that's been done since the last war," said the very up-to-date lady.

"You've got the wrong date: I'm against everything that's been done since Adam."

§

Hitler is without a doubt the most sinister character in history. And the most pathetic. He managed to achieve precisely the opposite of what he wanted, he destroyed his ideal point by point. It is for this reason that he is a monster in a class by himself—that is, a monster twice over, for even his pathos is monstrous.

§

All great events have been set in motion by madmen, by mediocre madmen. Which will be true, we may be sure, of the "end of the world" itself.

§

The Zohar teaches that those who do evil on earth were no better in heaven, that they were impatient to leave it, and, rushing to the mouth of the abyss, that they "arrived ahead of the time when they were to descend into this world."

One readily discerns the profundity of this vision of the pre-existence of souls, and its usefulness when we are to explain the assurance and the triumph of the "wicked," their solidity and their competence. Having prepared their endeavors so far ahead, it is not astonishing that they should possess the earth: they conquered it before they were here . . . , an eternity ago, and for all eternity, as a matter of fact.

§

What distinguishes the true prophet from the rest is that he stands at the origin of movements and doctrines which exclude and oppose each other.

§

In a metropolis as in a hamlet, what we still love best is to watch the fall of one of our kind.

§

The appetite for destruction is so deeply anchored within us that no one manages to extirpate it. It belongs to our constitution, for the very basis of our being is demoniac.

The sage is a pacified, withdrawn destroyer. The others are destroyers *in practice*.

§

Misfortune is a passive, endured state, while malediction supposes an election *à rebours*, consequently a notion of mission, of inner power, which is not implied in misfortune. An accursed individual or nation necessarily outclasses an unfortunate individual or nation.

§

Strictly speaking, history does not repeat itself, but since the illusions man is capable of are limited in number, they always return in another disguise, thereby giving some ultradecrepit filth a look of novelty and a tragic glaze.

§.

I read some pages on Jovinian, Saint Basil, and several others. The conflict, during the first centuries of Christianity, between orthodoxy and heresy seems no more insane than the one to which modern ideologies have accustomed us. The modalities of the controversy, the passions at work, the follies and the absurdities, are almost identical. In both cases, everything turns on the unreal and the unverifiable, which form the very basis of either religious or political dogmas. History would be tolerable only if we escaped both kinds. True, it would then cease altogether, for the great good of everyone—those who endure it as well as those who make it.

§

What makes destruction suspect is its facility: anyone who comes along can excel in it. But if to destroy is easy, to destroy oneself is less so. Superiority of the outcast over the agitator or the anarchist.

§

Had I lived in the early period of Christianity, I too, I fear, would have yielded to its seduction. And I hate that sympathizer, that hypothetical fanatic: I cannot forgive myself that conversion of two thousand years ago. . . .

§

Torn between violence and disillusionment, I seem to myself a terrorist who, going out in the street to perpetrate some outrage, stops on the way to consult Ecclesiastes or Epictetus.

§

According to Hegel, man will be completely free only "by surrounding himself with a world entirely created by himself."

But this is precisely what he has done, and man has never been so enchained, so much a slave as now.

§

Life would become endurable only among a humanity which would no longer have any illusions in reserve, a humanity completely disabused and *delighted* to be so.

§

Everything I have been able to feel and to think coincides with an exercise in anti-utopia.

§

Man will not last. Ambushed by exhaustion, he will have to pay for his too-original career. For it would be inconceivable and *contra naturam* that he drag on much longer and come to a good end. This prospect is depressing, hence likely.

§

"Enlightened despotism": the only regime that can attract a disabused mind, one incapable of being the accomplice of revolutions since it is not even the accomplice of history.

§

Nothing more painful than two *contemporary* prophets. One must withdraw, must disappear if he is unwilling to expose himself to ridicule. Unless both are thus exposed, which would be the most equitable solution.

§

I am stirred, even overwhelmed each time I happen upon an *innocent* person. Where does he come from? What is he after? Doesn't such an apparition herald some disaster? It is a very special disturbance we suffer in the presence of someone there is no way of calling our *kind*.

§

Wherever civilized men appeared for the first time, they were regarded by the natives as devils, as ghosts, specters. Never as *living men!* Unequaled intuition, a prophetic insight, if ever there was one.

§

If everyone had seen through everything, if everyone had "understood," history would have ceased long since. But we are fundamentally, biologically unsuited to "understand." And even if everyone understood except for one, history would be perpetuated because of that one, because of his blindness. Because of a *single* illusion!

§

X maintains we are at the end of a "cosmic cycle" and that soon everything will fall apart. And he does not doubt this for one moment.

At the same time, he is the father of a—numerous—family. With certitudes like his, what aberration has deluded him into bringing into a doomed world one child after the next? If we foresee the End, if we are sure it will be coming soon, if we even anticipate it, better to do so alone. One does not procreate on Patmos.

§

Montaigne, a sage, has had no posterity. Rousseau, an hysteric, still stirs nations. I like only the thinkers who have inspired no tribune of the people.

§

In 1441, the Council of Florence decreed that pagans, Jews, heretics, and schismatics will have no part in "eternal life" and that all, unless they embrace, before dying, the true religion, will go straight to hell.

In the days when the Church professed such enormities it was truly the Church. An institution is vital and strong only if it rejects everything which is not itself. Unfortunately the same is true of a nation or of a regime.

§

A serious, honest mind understands—and can understand—nothing of history. History in return is marvelously suited to delight an erudite cynic.

§

Extraordinary pleasure at the thought that, being human, one is born under an accursed star, and that whatever one has undertaken and whatever one is going to undertake will be fondled by mischance.

§

Plotinus befriended a Roman senator who had freed his slaves, renounced his wealth, and who ate and slept at the houses of friends, for he no longer owned anything. This senator, from the "official" point of view, was deranged, and his case would be regarded as distressing, which indeed it was: a *saint* in the Senate. . . . His presence, even his possibility—what an omen! The hordes were not far. . . .

§

A man who has completely vanquished selfishness, who retains no trace of it whatever, cannot live longer than twenty-one days, according to one modern Vedantist school. No Western moralist, not even the grimmest, would have dared venture an observation on human nature so startling, so revealing.

§

We invoke "progress" less and less and "mutation" more and more, and all that we allege to illustrate the latter's advantages is merely one symptom after another of an unrivaled catastrophe.

§

We can breathe—and brawl—only in a corrupt regime. But we realize as much only after having contributed to its destruction, and when nothing is left but our capacity to regret it.

§

What we call the creative instinct is merely a deviation, merely a perversion of our nature: we have not been brought into the world in order to innovate, to revolutionize, but to enjoy our semblance of being, in order to liquidate it quietly and to vanish afterward without a fuss.

§

The Aztecs were right to believe the gods must be appeased, to offer them human blood every day in order to keep the universe from sinking back into chaos.

We long since ceased to believe in the gods, and we no longer offer them sacrifices. Yet the world is still here. No doubt. Only we no longer have the good luck to know why it does not collapse on the spot.

9

We pursue whatever we pursue out of torment—a need for torment. Our very quest for salvation is a torment, the subtlest, the best camouflaged of all.

§

If it is true that by death we once more become what we were before being, would it not have been better to abide by that pure possibility, not to stir from it? What use was this detour, when we might have remained forever in an unrealized plenitude?

§

Once my body gives me the slip, how, I wonder, with such carrion on my hands, will I combat the capitulation of my organs?

§

The ancient gods ridiculed men, envied them, hunted them down on occasion, harried them. The God of the Gospels was less mocking and less jealous, and mortal men did not even enjoy, in their miseries, the consolation of being able to accuse Him. Which accounts for the absence or the impossibility of a Christian Aeschylus. A *good* God has killed tragedy. Zeus deserved differently of literature.

§

Haunted, obsessed by abdication, as far back as I can remember. But abdication of what? If I once longed to be "someone," it was only for the satisfaction of someday being able to say, like Charles V at Yuste: "I am no longer anything."

§

Some of the *Provincial Letters* were rewritten as many as seventeen times. Astounding that Pascal could have expended so much time and energy whose interest seems minimal to us now. Every polemic dates—every polemic with men. In the *Pensées*, the debate was with God. This still concerns us somewhat.

§

Saint Seraphim of Sarov, in his fifteen years of complete seclusion, opened his cell door to no one, not even to the bishop who occasionally visited the hermitage. "Silence," he would say, "brings man closer to God and makes him, on earth, like unto the angels."

What the saint should have added is that silence is never deeper than in the impossibility of prayer. . . .

§

Modern man has lost the sense of fate and thereby the savor of lamentation. In the theater we should reinstate the chorus at once, and at funerals, the mourners. . . .

§

In anxiety, a man clings to whatever can reinforce, can stimulate his providential discomfort: to try to cure him of it is to destroy his equilibrium, anxiety being the basis of his existence and his prosperity. The cunning confessor knows it is necessary, knows that we cannot do without anxiety once we have known it. Since he dares not proclaim its benefits, he employs a detour—he vaunts remorse, an admitted, an honorable anxiety. His customers are grateful; hence he manages to keep them readily enough, whereas his lay colleagues struggle and grovel to keep theirs.

§

You once told me death did not exist. Agreed, provided you add that nothing exists. To grant reality to anything and to deny it to what seems so manifestly real is sheer extravagance.

§

When we have committed the folly of confiding a secret to someone, the only way of being sure he will keep it to himself is to kill him on the spot.

§

"Sicknesses, some by day, others by night, in their fashion, visit men, bearing suffering to mortals—in silence, for wise Zeus has denied them speech" (Hesiod).

Fortunately, for, being mute, they are already excruciating— what would they be if they were garrulous as well? Can we imagine even one *proclaiming itself*? Instead of symptoms, declarations! Zeus, for once, has shown signs of delicacy.

§

In periods of sterility, one should hibernate, sleep day and night to preserve one's strength, instead of wasting it in mortification and rage.

§

We can admire someone only if he is three-quarters irresponsible—admiration has nothing to do with respect.

§

The not at all negligible advantage of having greatly hated men is that one comes to endure them by the exhaustion of this very hatred.

§

Once the shutters are closed, I stretch out in the dark. The outer world, a fading murmur, dissolves. All that is left is myself and . . . there's the rub. Hermits have spent their lives in dialogue with what was most hidden within them. If only, following their example, I could give myself up to that extreme exercise, in which one unites with the intimacy of one's own being! It is this self-interview, this inward transition which matters, and which has no value unless continually renewed, so that the self is finally absorbed by its essential version.

§

Even in God's company, discontent was brewing, as the revolt of the angels testifies—the first on record. Apparently on every level of creation, no one is forgiven his superiority. We might even conceive of an *envious* flower.

§

The virtues have no face. Impersonal, abstract, conventional, they wear out faster than the vices, which, more powerfully charged with vitality, define themselves and become accentuated with age.

§

"Everything is filled with gods," said Thales, at the dawn of philosophy; at the other end, at this twilight we have come to, we can proclaim, not only out of a need for symmetry but even more out of respect for the evidence, that "everything is emptied of gods."

§

I was alone in that cemetery overlooking the village when a pregnant woman came in. I left at once, in order not to look at this corpse-bearer at close range, nor to ruminate upon the contrast between an aggressive womb and the time-worn tombs—between a false promise and the end of all promises.

§

The desire to pray has nothing to do with faith. It emanates from a special despondency, and lasts as long, even while the gods and their very memory may vanish away forever.

§

"No language can hope for anything but its own defeat" (Gregory Palamas).

So radical a condemnation of all literature could come only from a mystic—from a professional of the Inexpressible.

§

In Antiquity, one resorted readily, especially among the philosophers, to voluntary asphyxia—one held one's breath until . . . one died. So elegant and yet so practical a mode of being done with it has completely disappeared, and it is anything but certain it can ever reappear.

§

It has been said and said again: the concept of destiny, which supposes change, history, does not apply to an immutable being. Hence we cannot speak of God's "destiny."

Doubtless we cannot, in theory. In practice, we do nothing but, particularly in the periods when beliefs are dissolving, when faith is shaky, when nothing seems able to withstand time, when God Himself is swept into the general deliquescence.

§

Once we begin to *want*, we fall under the jurisdiction of the Devil.

§

Life is nothing; death, everything. Yet there *is* nothing which is death, independent of life. It is precisely this absence of autonomous, distinct reality which makes death universal; it has no realm of its own, it is omnipresent, like everything which lacks identity, limit, and bearing: an indecent infinitude.

§

Euphoria. Incapable of articulating my habitual moods and the reflections they engender, impelled by some unknown power, I exulted without motive, and it is just such jubilation, of unknown origin, I reminded myself, which is the experience of those who do and strive, those who *produce*. They neither can nor will reflect on what denies them. And if they did, it would be of no consequence, as was the case for me that memorable day.

§

Why embroider upon what excludes commentary? A text explained is no longer a text. We live with an idea, we don't dissect it; we struggle with it, we don't describe the stages of the conflict. The history of philosophy is the negation of philosophy.

§

A suspect scruple led me to wonder exactly what it was by which I was fatigued, and I began drawing up the list: though incomplete, it appeared so long, and so depressing, that I decided to fall back on *fatigue in itself*, a flattering formula which, thanks to its philosophical ingredient, might restore a plague victim.

§

Destruction and explosion of syntax, victory of ambiguity and approximation. All very well. But just try to draw up a will, and you'll see if the defunct rigor was so contemptible.

§

An aphorism? Fire without flames. Understandable that no one tries to warm himself at it.

§

Even if I were to lose my reason, I could never bring myself to that "uninterrupted prayer" advocated by the Hesychasts. All I understand about piety is its excesses, its suspect outrages, and *askesis* would not interest me a moment if one did not encounter there all those things which are the lot of the bad monk: indolence, gluttony, the thirst for desolation, greed, and aversion for the world, vacillation between tragedy and the equivocal, hope of an inner collapse. . . .

§

I forget which Father recommends manual labor against acedia. Admirable advice, which I have always followed spontaneously: no depression, that secular acedia, can resist puttering.

§

Years now without coffee, without alcohol, without tobacco. . . . Luckily, there is anxiety, which usefully replaces the strongest stimulants.

§

The worst reproach to be made against police states is that they oblige—for prudence's sake—the destruction of letters and diaries, i.e., what is least false in literature.

§

To keep the mind alert, slander turns out to be as effective as disease: the same vigilance, the same fixed attention, the same insecurity, the same flagellating hysteria, the same mortal enrichment.

§

I am nothing, obviously, but since for so long I wanted to be something, I fail to smother that aspiration, that will: it exists because it has existed, it belabors me and prevails, though I reject it. Try as I do to relegate it to my past, it kicks up again and torments me: never having been satisfied, it has maintained itself intact, and has no intention of yielding to my orders. Caught between my will and myself, what can I do?

§

In his *Ladder of Paradise*, Saint John Climacus notes that a proud monk has no need to be persecuted by the Devil—he is himself his own devil.

I think of X, whose life in the monastery was a failure. No one was better constituted to distinguish himself in the world and to shine there. Unsuited to humility, to obedience, he chose solitude and bogged down in it. There was nothing in him to become, according to the same saint's expression, "the lover of God." Out of irony one can neither create one's own salvation nor help others create theirs; one can merely disguise one's wounds, if not one's distastes.

§

It is a great force, and a great fortune, to be able to live without any ambition whatever. I aspire to it, but the very fact of so aspiring still participates in ambition.

§

The blank time of meditation is, in truth, the only "full" time. We should never blush to accumulate vacant moments—vacant in appearance, filled in fact. To meditate is a supreme leisure, whose secret has been lost.

§

Noble gestures are always suspect. Each time, we regret having committed them. Something false about them, something theatrical, attitudinizing. It is true that we regret ignoble gestures almost as much.

§

If I reflect on any moment of my life, the most feverish or the most neutral, what remains?—and what difference is there now between them? Everything having become the same, without relief and without reality, it is when I *felt nothing* that I was closest to the truth, I mean to my present state in which I am recapitulating my experiences. What is the use of having felt anything at all? There is no "ecstasy" which either memory or imagination can resuscitate!

§

No one, before his last moment, manages to *use up* his death altogether: even for the born moribund, death has a touch of novelty.

§

According to the Cabbala, God created souls at the beginning, and they were all before him in the form they would later take in their incarnation. Each soul, when its time has come, receives the order to join the body destined for it, but each to no avail implores its Creator to spare it this bondage and this corruption.

The more I think of what could not have failed to happen when my own soul's turn came, the more I realize that if there was one soul which more than the rest must have resisted incarnation, it was mine.

§

We dismiss the skeptic, we speak of an "automatism of doubt," while we never say of a believer that he has fallen into an "automatism of faith." Yet faith is much more mechanical than doubt, which has the excuse of proceeding from surprise to surprise—inside perplexity, it is true.

§

That faint light in each of us which dates back to before our birth, to before all births, is what must be protected if we want to rejoin that remote glory from which we shall never know why we were separated.

§

I have never known a single sensation of fulfillment, of true happiness, without thinking that it was the moment when—now or never—I should disappear for good.

§

A moment comes when it seems futile to have to choose between metaphysics and amateurism, between the unfathomable and the anecdote.

§

To measure accurately the decline Christianity represents in relation to paganism, we need merely compare the pathetic remarks of the Church Fathers on suicide with the opinions offered on the same subject by a Pliny, a Seneca, and even a Cicero.

§

What is the point of what we say? Is there any meaning to this series of propositions which constitutes our talk? And do these propositions, taken one by one, have any object? We can talk only if we set aside this question, or if we raise it as infrequently as possible.

§

"To hell with *everything*"—if these words have been uttered, even only once, coldly, with complete awareness of what they mean, history is justified and, with it, all of us.

§

"Woe unto you, when all men speak well of you!" Christ was here foretelling his own end. All men now speak well of him, even the most hardened unbelievers—they above all. Jesus knew perfectly well that he would one day succumb to universal approbation.

Christianity is lost if it does not suffer persecutions as pitiless as those it was subjected to at its beginning. It must provoke enemies at all costs, prepare great calamities for itself. Only a new Nero might still be able to save it.

§

I believe speech to be a recent invention, and find it hard to imagine a dialogue that dates back beyond ten thousand years. And even harder, a dialogue that will occur in not ten thousand but even a thousand years from now.

§

In a work of psychiatry, only the patients' remarks interest me; in a work of criticism, only the quotations.

§

No one can do anything for this Polish woman, who is beyond sickness and health, even beyond living and dying. A phantom cannot be cured, still less an enlightened mind. We can cure only those who belong to the earth and still have their roots in it, however superficial.

§

The periods of sterility we pass through coincide with an exacerbation of our discernment—with the eclipse of the madman in us.

§

To proceed to the extremities of one's art and, even further, of one's being: such is the law of any man who regards himself to any degree as *chosen*.

§

It is because of speech that men give the illusion of being free. If they did—without a word—what they do, we would take them for robots. By speaking, they deceive themselves, as they deceive others: because they say what they are going to do, who could suspect they are not masters of their actions?

§

Deep inside, each man feels—and believes—himself to be immortal, even if he knows he will perish the next moment. We can understand everything, admit everything, *realize* everything, except our death, even when we ponder it unremittingly and even when we are resigned to it.

§

In the slaughterhouse that morning, I watched the cattle being led to their death. Almost every animal, at the last moment, refused to move forward. To make them do so, a man hit them on the hind legs.

This scene often comes to mind when, ejected from sleep, I lack the strength to confront the daily torture of Time.

§

I pride myself on my capacity to perceive the transitory character of everything. An odd gift which has spoiled all my joys; better: all my sensations.

§

Everyone expiates his first moment.

§

For an instant, I think I experienced what absorption into Brahma might signify for an adept of the Vedanta. How much I longed for that instant to be extensible—infinitely!

§

I sought in doubt a remedy for anxiety. The remedy ended by making common cause with the disease.

§

"If a doctrine spreads, it is because heaven has so desired" (Confucius).

. . . As I should like to believe each time that, faced with some victorious aberration, my rage borders on apoplexy.

§

The number of fanatics, extremists, and degenerates I have been able to admire! A relief bordering on orgasm at the notion that one will never again embrace a cause, any cause . . .

§

An acrobat? An orchestra conductor caught up by the Idea? He rushes in, then calms down, alternates the allegro with the andante, a master of himself like the fakirs or the swindlers. While he is talking, he seems to be seeking something, but one never knows what: an expert in the art of counterfeiting the thinker. If he were to say a single thing that was perfectly clear, he would be lost. Since he is as ignorant as his hearers of what he wants to say or what he wants, he can go on for hours without exhausting the amazement of the puppets listening to him.

§

A privilege to live in conflict with one's times. At every moment one is aware one does not think like the others. This state of acute dissimilarity, however indigent or sterile it appears, nonetheless possesses a philosophical status which one would be at a loss to seek in cogitations attuned to events.

§

"There's no help for it," the nonagenarian kept repeating to whatever I said, to whatever I shouted into her ear concerning the present, the future, the march of events. . . .

In the hope of getting some other response from her, I went on with my apprehensions, my grievances, my complaints. Obtaining only the sempiternal "No help for it," I came to the end of my patience and left, irritated with myself, irritated with her. What folly, to confide in an idiot!

Outside, complete reversal: "But the old woman's right. How could I fail to realize right away that her refrain had a truth in it, doubtless the most important truth of all, since everything that happens proclaims it and everything in ourselves rejects it?"

10

Two kinds of intuitions: original (Homer, Upanishads, folklore) and belated (Mahayana Buddhism, Roman stoicism, Alexandrian gnosis). First flashes and fading glows. The wakening of consciousness and the lassitude of being awakened.

§

If it is true that what perishes has never existed, birth, source of the perishable, exists as little as the rest.

§

Beware of euphemisms! They aggravate the horror they are supposed to disguise. To use, as the French do, "the disappeared" instead of *the deceased* or *the dead man,* seems to me preposterous, even insane.

§

When man forgets he is mortal, he feels inclined to do great things, and sometimes succeeds. This oblivion, fruit of excess, is at the same time the cause of his woes. "Mortal, think as a mortal." Antiquity invented a *tragic modesty.*

§

Of all the equestrian statues of Roman emperors, the only one to survive the barbarian invasions and the erosion of the ages is that of Marcus Aurelius—the least "emperor" of all and the one who would have adapted himself to any other condition.

§

Getting up with my head full of plans, I would be working, I was sure of it, all morning long. No sooner had I sat down at my desk than the odious, vile, and persuasive refrain: "What do you expect of this world?" stopped me short. And I returned, as usual, to my bed with the hope of finding some answer, of going back to sleep. . . .

§

We make choices, decisions, as long as we keep to the surface of things; once we reach the depths, we can neither choose nor decide, we can do nothing but regret the surface. . . .

§

The fear of being deceived is the vulgar version of the quest for Truth.

§

When you know yourself well and do not despise yourself utterly, it is because you are too exhausted to indulge in extreme feelings.

§

It is a withering process to follow a doctrine, a belief, a system—for a writer especially; unless he lives, as often happens, in contradiction with the ideas to which he appeals. This contradiction, or this treason, stimulates him and keeps him in a state of insecurity, embarrassment, shame—conditions favorable to production.

§

Paradise was the place where everything was known but where nothing was explained. The universe before sin—before *commentary* . . .

§

I have no faith, luckily. If I had, I should live in constant fear of losing it. Hence, far from helping me, it would do nothing but injure me.

§

An impostor, a "humbug," conscious of being so and therefore a self-spectator, is necessarily more advanced in knowledge than a steady mind full of merits and all of a piece.

§

Anyone possessing a body is entitled to be called a reprobate. If he is afflicted with a "soul" as well, there is no anathema to which he cannot lay claim.

§

How are we to speak to someone who has lost everything? What language shall we use? The most diffuse, the vaguest, will always be the most effective.

§

Supremacy of regret: the actions we have not performed

constitute, by the very fact that they pursue us and that we continually think about them, the sole contents of our consciousness.

§

Sometimes I wish I were a cannibal—less for the pleasure of eating someone than for the pleasure of vomiting him.

§

No longer wanting to be a man . . . , dreaming of another form of failure.

§

Each time you find yourself at a turning-point, the best thing is to lie down and let the hours pass. Resolutions made standing up are worthless: they are dictated either by pride or by fear. Prone, we still know these two scourges, but in a more attenuated, more intemporal form.

§

When someone complains that his life has come to nothing, we need merely remind him that life itself is in an analogous situation, if not worse.

§

Works die: fragments, not having lived, cannot die either.

§

Horror of the accessory paralyzes me. Now, the accessory is the essence of communication (and hence of thought), it is the flesh and blood of speech and writing. Trying to renounce it is like fornicating with a skeleton.

§

The satisfaction we take from performing a task (especially when we have no belief in the task and even disdain it) shows to what degree we still belong to the rabble.

§

My merit is not to be totally ineffectual but to have wanted to be.

§

If I do not deny my origins, it is because it is ultimately better to be nothing at all than a pretense of something.

§

A mixture of automatism and whim, man is a robot with defects, a robot *out of order*. If only he remains so, and is not some day *put right!*

§

What every man, whether he has patience or not, has always expected is, of course, death. But he knows this only when death comes . . . , when it is too late to be able to enjoy it.

§

Man certainly began praying long before he knew how to speak, for the pangs he must have suffered upon leaving animality, upon denying it, could not have been endured without grunts and groans, prefigurations, premonitory signs of prayer.

§

In art and in everything, the commentator is generally better informed and more lucid than the subject of commentary. This is the advantage the murderer has over his victim.

§

"Let us offer our thanks to the gods, who keep no one in this life by force." Seneca (whose style, according to Caligula, lacks *cement*) is open to the essential, and this not so much because of his affiliation with stoicism as because of his eight-years' exile in Corsica, particularly desolate at the time. This ordeal conferred upon a frivolous writer a dimension he would not have acquired in the normal course of events; it relieved him of the aid of a sickness.

§

Mine still, this moment passes by, escapes me, and is buried forever. Am I going to commit myself with the next? I make up my mind: it is here, it belongs to me—and already is long since past. From morning to night, fabricating the past!

§

After having, to no avail, tried everything among the mystics, he had only one recourse: to founder in wisdom. . . .

§

Once you ask yourself so-called philosophical questions and employ the inevitable jargon, you assume a superior, aggressive manner, and this in a realm where, the insoluble being *de rigueur,* humility should be also. This anomaly is merely apparent: the more formidable the questions you confront, the more you lose your head: ultimately you bestow on yourself the dimensions they possess. If the pride of theologians "stinks" even more than that of the philosophers, it is because one does not concern oneself with God with impunity: one reaches the point of arrogating to oneself certain of His attributes—the worst, of course.

§

At peace with itself and the world, the mind atrophies. It flourishes at the slightest contrariety. Thought is really no more than the shameless exploitation of our embarrassments and our disgraces.

§

This body, once loyal, disavows me, no longer follows me, has ceased to be my accomplice. Rejected, betrayed, discarded, what would become of me if old infirmities, to prove their allegiance, didn't come to keep me company at every hour of the day and night?

§

"Distinguished" people do not invent in matters of language. On the contrary, the ones who excel there are those who improvise out of boastfulness or who wallow in a sentimental coarseness. Such men are "natures," they live on the level of words. Is verbal genius, then, the concomitant of low haunts? In any case, it requires a certain minimum of odium.

§

We should keep to a single language, and deepen our knowledge of it at every opportunity. For a writer, gossiping with a concierge in his own is much more profitable than arguing with a scholar in a foreign tongue.

§

". . . the feeling of being everything and the evidence of being nothing." I happened across this phrase in my youth, and was overwhelmed by it. Everything I felt in those days, and everything I would feel from then on, was summed up in this extraordinary banal formula, the synthesis of expansion and failure, ecstasy and impasse. Most often it is not in a paradox but in a truism that a revelation appears.

§

Poetry excludes calculation and premeditation: it is incompletion, foreboding, abyss. Neither a singsong geometry, nor a succession of bloodless adjectives. We are too deeply wounded and too despondent, too weary and too barbarous in our weariness, to appreciate, yet, the *craft*.

§

We cannot do without the notion of progress, yet it does not deserve our attention. It is like the "meaning" of life. Life *must* have one. But is there any which does not turn out, upon examination, to be ludicrous?

§

Trees are massacred, houses go up—faces, faces everywhere. Man is *spreading*. Man is the cancer of the earth.

§

There is something enveloping and voluptuous about the notion of fatality: it keeps you warm.

§

A troglodyte that will have passed through all the nuances of satiety. . . .

§

The pleasure of slandering yourself greatly exceeds that of being slandered.

§

Better than anyone I know the danger of being born with a thirst for everything. A poisoned gift, a vengeance of Providence. Thus encumbered, I could get nowhere, on the spiritual level, of course, the only one that matters. Anything but accidental, my failure is identified with my essence.

§

The mystics and their "collected works." When one addresses oneself to God, and to God alone, as they claim to do, one should be careful not to write. God doesn't *read*. . . .

§

Each time I think of the Essential, I seem to glimpse it in silence or explosion, in stupor or exclamation. Never in speech.

§

When you meditate all day on the inopportuneness of birth, everything you plan and everything you perform seems pathetic, futile. You are like a madman who, cured, does nothing but think of the crisis from which he has emerged, the "dream" he has left behind; he keeps harking back to it, so that his cure is of no benefit to him whatever.

§

The appetite for torment is for some what the lure of gain is for others.

§

Man started out on the wrong foot. The misadventure in Paradise was the first consequence. The rest had to follow.

§

I shall never understand how we can live knowing that we are not—to say the least!—eternal.

§

The ideal being? An angel ravaged by humor.

§

When, after a series of questions about desire, disgust, and serenity, Buddha was asked: "What is the goal, the final meaning of nirvana?" he did not answer. He *smiled*. There has been a great deal of commentary on that smile, instead of seeing it as a normal reaction to a pointless question. It is what we do when confronted by a child's *why*. We smile, because no answer is conceivable, because the answer would be even more meaningless than the question. Children admit no limits to anything; they always want to see beyond, to see what there is afterward. But there is no afterward. Nirvana is a limit, the limit. It is liberation, supreme impasse. . . .

§

Existence might well have had some attraction before the advent of noise—let us say, before the neolithic age. When will he come, the man who can rid us of all men?

§

For all we tell ourselves about not outliving a stillborn babe, instead of clearing out at the first opportunity, we cling, with lunatic energy, to one day more.

§

Lucidity does not extirpate the desire to live—far from it, lucidity merely makes us unsuited to life.

§

God: a disease we imagine we are cured of because no one dies of it nowadays.

§

Unconsciousness is the secret, the "vital principle" of life. . . . It is the sole recourse against the self, against the disease of being individualized, against the debilitating effect of the state of consciousness, a state so formidable, so demanding, that it must be reserved for athletes alone.

§

Any success, in any realm, involves an inner impoverishment. It makes us forget what we are, it deprives us of the torment of our limits.

§

I have never taken myself for a *being*. A non-citizen, a marginal type, a nothing who exists only by the excess, by the superabundance of his nothingness.

§

To have foundered somewhere between the epigram and the sigh!

§

Suffering opens our eyes, helps us to see what we would not have seen otherwise. Hence it is useful only to knowledge and, except for that, serves only to poison existence. Which, one may add in passing, favors knowledge further. "He has suffered—hence he has understood." This is all we can say of a victim of disease, injustice, or of any kind of misfortune. Suffering improves no one (except those who were already *good*), it is forgotten as all things are forgotten, it does not enter into "humanity's patrimony" nor preserve itself in any way at all—it wastes itself as everything is wasted. Once again, it serves only to open our eyes.

§

Man has said what he had to say. He should rest now. But refuses, and though he has entered into his "survivor" phase, he fidgets as if he were on the threshold of an astonishing career.

§

A cry means something only in a created universe. If there is no creator, what is the good of calling attention to yourself?

§

Nerval: "Having reached the Place de la Concorde, my thought was to kill myself." Nothing in all French literature has haunted me as much as that.

§

In everything, only the beginning and the outcome matter, doing and undoing. The way toward being and the way out of being—that is breathing, whereas being as such is merely an asphyxiator.

§

With the passage of time, I am convinced that my first years were a paradise. But I am undoubtedly mistaken. If there was ever a paradise, I must look for it earlier than all my years.

§

A golden rule: to leave an incomplete image of oneself . . .

§

The more man is man, the more he loses in reality: it is the price he must pay for his distinct essence. If he managed to achieve the limits of his singularity, if he were to become man totally, absolutely, there would no longer be anything in him which would suggest any kind of existence at all.

§

Silence in the face of the decrees of fate, the rediscovery, after centuries of thundering prayer, of the ancient *Be still*—there is our aspiration, there our struggle, if such a word is appropriate to a foreseen and accepted defeat.

§

Every success is ignominious; we never get over it—in our own eyes, of course.

§

The pangs of truth about ourselves are more than we can endure. How pitiable the man (if such a being exists) who no longer lies to himself!

§

I shall no longer read the sages—they have done me too much harm. I should have surrendered to my instincts, let my madness flourish. I have done just the opposite, I have put on the mask of reason, and the mask has ended by replacing my face and usurping all the rest.

§

In my moments, of megalomania, I tell myself that it is impossible my diagnoses should be mistaken, that I have only to be patient, to wait until the end, until the advent of the last man, the one being in a position to substantiate me. . . .

§

The notion that it would have been better never to exist is among those which meet with the most opposition. Every man, incapable of seeing himself except from inside, regards himself as necessary, even indispensable, every man feels and perceives himself as an absolute reality, as a whole, as the whole. The moment we identify ourselves entirely with our own being, we react like God, we *are* God.

It is only when we live at once within and on the margins of ourselves that we can conceive, quite calmly, that it would have been preferable that the accident we are should never have occurred.

§

If I followed my natural inclination, I should blow up the world. And it is because I lack the courage to follow it that, out of penitence, I try to stupefy myself with the company of those who have found peace.

§

A writer has left his mark on us not because we have read him a great deal but because we have thought of him more than is warranted. I have not frequented Baudelaire or Pascal particularly, but I have not stopped thinking of their miseries, which have accompanied me everywhere as faithfully as my own.

§

At each age, more or less distinct signs warn us that it is time to decamp. We hesitate, we procrastinate, convinced that, once old age has come at last, these signs will become so clear that any further vacillation would be unsuitable. Clear they are, indeed, but we lack sufficient vigor to perform the one decent action a living man can commit.

§

The name of an actress famous in my childhood suddenly occurs to me. Who still remembers her? Much more than any philosophical meditation, it is details of this sort which reveal the scandalous reality and unreality of time.

§

If we manage to last in spite of everything, it is because our infirmities are so many and so contradictory that they cancel each other out.

§

The only moments I think of with relief are those when I sought to be nothing for anyone, when I blushed at the notion of leaving the slightest trace in the memory of a single human being. . . .

§

Indispensable condition for spiritual fulfillment: to have always placed the wrong bet.

§

If we hope to see the number of our disappointments or our frenzies diminish, then on every occasion we must remember that we are here to make each other wretched, and that to rebel against this state of affairs is to undermine the very foundations of communal life.

§

A disease is ours only from the moment we are told its name, the moment when the rope is put around our neck. . . . .

§

All my thoughts are turned toward resignation, and yet not a day passes when I fail to concoct some ultimatum to God or to anyone. . . .

§

When every man has realized that his birth is a defeat, existence, endurable at last, will seem like the day after a surrender, like the relief and the repose of the conquered.

§

As long as we believed in the Devil, everything that happened was intelligible and clear; now that we no longer do, we must look for a new explanation for each event, an accounting that will be as laborious as it is arbitrary, one which intrigues everyone and satisfies no one.

§

The Truth we do not always pursue; but when we do so passionately, violently, we hate whatever is *expression*, whatever derives from words and forms, all the noble lies, even further from the truth than the vulgar ones.

§

Only what proceeds from emotion or from cynicism is real. All the rest is "talent."

§

Vitality and rejection go hand in hand. Indulgence, a sign of anemia, suppresses laughter, since it bows before all forms of dissimilarity.

§

Our physiological miseries help us to envisage the future with some confidence: they dispense us from tormenting ourselves overmuch, they do their best so that none of our long-range projects has time to wear out all our available energies.

§

The Empire was falling, the Barbarians were on the move. . . . What was to be done, except to escape the age? Happy moment, when there was still somewhere to go, when the empty places were accessible and welcoming! We have been dispossessed of everything, even the desert.

§

For the man who has got in the nasty habit of unmasking appearances, *event* and *misunderstanding* are synonyms. To make for the essential is to throw up the game, to admit one is defeated.

§

X is undoubtedly right to compare himself to a "volcano," but wrong to go into details.

§

The poor, by thinking unceasingly of money, reach the point of losing the spiritual advantages of non-possession, thereby sinking as low as the rich.

§

The early Greeks regarded the psyche as no more than air, wind, or at best smoke, and one readily agrees with them every time one wearies of foraging in one's own ego or that of others, searching for strange and, if possible, suspect depths.

§

The final step toward indifference is the destruction of the very notion of indifference.

§

Walking in a forest between two hedges of ferns transfigured by autumn—that is a *triumph*. What are ovations and applause beside it?

§

To deprecate your own kind, to vilify and pulverize them, to attack their foundations, to undermine your very basis, to destroy your point of departure, to punish your origins . . . , to curse all those non-elect, lesser breeds, torn between imposture and elegy, whose sole mission is not to have one . . .

§

Having destroyed all my connections, burned my bridges, I should feel a certain freedom, and in fact I do, one so intense I am afraid to rejoice in it.

§

When the habit of seeing things as they are turns into a mania, we lament the madman we have been and are no longer.

11

Someone we regard highly comes closer to us when he performs an action unworthy of him—thereby he releases us from the calvary of veneration. And starting from that moment we feel a true attachment to him.

§

Nothing is worse than the coarseness and meanness we perpetrate out of timidity.

§

Faced with the Nile and the Pyramids, Flaubert thought of nothing but Normandy, according to one witness—nothing but the landscapes and manners of the future *Madame Bovary*. Nothing but that seemed to exist for him. To imagine is to limit oneself, to exclude: without an excessive capacity for rejection, no plan, no work, no way of *realizing* anything.

§

What in any way resembles a victory seems to me so dishonorable that I can do battle, in whatever circumstance, only with the firm intention of gaining the under hand. I have passed the stage where beings matter, and I see no reason to struggle in known worlds.

§

Philosophy is taught only in the agora, in a garden, or at home. The lecture chair is the grave of philosophy, the death of any living thought, the dais is the mind in mourning.

§

That I can still desire proves that I lack an exact perception of reality, that I am distracted, that I am a thousand miles from the Truth. "Man," we read in the *Dhammapada*, "is prey to desire only because he does not see things as they are."

§

I was shaking with rage: my honor was at stake. The hours passed, dawn was approaching. Was I going to ruin my night because of a trifle? Try as I would to minimize the incident, the reasons I invented to calm myself remained ineffectual. That anyone would dare do such a thing to me! I was on the point of opening the window and screaming like a madman, when the image of our planet spinning like a top suddenly seized my mind. My anger subsided at once.

§

Death is not altogether useless: after all, it is because of death that we may be able to recuperate the prenatal space, our only space. . . .

§

How right it was to begin the day, as men once did, with a prayer, a call for help! Ignorant of whom to address ourselves to, we will end by groveling before the first cracked god to come along.

§

Acute consciousness of having a body—that is the absence of health. . . . Which is as much as to say that I have never been well.

§

Everything is deception—I've always known that. Yet this certitude has afforded me no relief, except at the moments when it was violently present to my mind. . . .

§

The perception of the Precarious raised to the level of vision, of mystical experience.

§

The only way of enduring one disaster after the next is to love the very idea of disaster: if we succeed, there are no further surprises, we are superior to whatever occurs, we are invincible victims.

§

In very powerful sensations of pain, much more than in very slight ones, we observe ourselves, we divide into an external witness and the moaning, screaming sufferer. Everything which borders on torment wakens the psychologist in each of us, as well as the experimenter: we want to see how far we can go in the intolerable.

§

What is injustice compared to disease? True, we may find it unjust to be sick. Moreover that is how each of us reacts, without troubling as to whether he is right or wrong. Sickness *is:* nothing more real than disease. If we call it unjust, we must dare to do as much with Being itself—we must speak, then, of the *injustice of existing.*

§

The Creation, as it was, amounted to little enough; tinkered with, it was worth still less. If only it had been left to its truth, its primal nullity! The Messiah to come—the real one—is understandably slow about putting in an appearance. The task that awaits him is not going to be an easy one: how will he manage to deliver humanity from the *mania of amelioration?*

§

When, getting too used to ourselves, we begin to loathe ourselves, we soon realize that we are worse off, that self-hatred actually strengthens self-attachment.

§

I do not interrupt him, I let him weigh each man's merits, waiting for him to tell me off. . . . His incomprehension of others is astounding. Subtle and ingenuous both, he judges you as if you were an entity or a category. Time having had no hold over him, he cannot admit that I am outside of whatever he forbids, that nothing of what he favors still concerns me. Dialogue becomes pointless with someone who escapes the procession of the years. I ask those I love to be kind enough to grow old.

§

Panic in the face of anything—of presence, of the void, of anything. *Original* panic.

§

God *is*, even if He isn't.

§

D is incapable of assimilating Evil. He acknowledges its existence, but cannot incorporate it into his mind. If he were to emerge from hell he would be oblivious of his whereabouts, so remote is he in his thinking from what falls afoul. . . . Not the faintest trace of all he has endured in his ideas. Occasionally he has reflexes—no more than that—the reflexes of a wounded man. Closed to the negative, he does not discern that all we possess is merely a capital of non-being. Yet more than one of his gestures reveals a demonic spirit—demonic unawares. He is a destroyer obscured and sterilized by Good.

§

Curiosity to measure our progress into failure is the only reason we have to grow older. We thought we had reached the limit, we thought the horizon was blocked forever, we lamented in the thrall of our discouragement. And now we realize that we can fall still lower, that there is something new, that all hope is not lost, that it is possible to sink a little further and thus to postpone the danger of getting stuck, even paralyzed. . . .

§

"Life seems good only to the madman," observed Hegesias, a Cyrenaic philosopher, some twenty-three centuries ago. These are almost the only words of his we have. . . . Of all oeuvres to reinvent, his comes first on my list.

§

No one approaches the condition of a *sage* if he has not had the good luck to be forgotten in his lifetime.

§

To think is to undermine—to undermine *oneself*. Action involves fewer risks, for it fills the interval between things and ourselves, whereas reflection dangerously widens it.

. . . So long as I give myself up to physical exercise, manual labor, I am happy, fulfilled; once I stop, I am seized by dizziness, and I can think of nothing but giving up for good.

§

At the lowest point of ourselves, when we touch bottom and *feel* the abyss, we are suddenly raised up—defense-reaction or absurd pride—by the sense of being *superior* to God. The grandiose and impure aspect of the temptation to be done with it all.

§

A broadcast about wolves, with recordings of their howls. What a language! The most heartrending I know, and I shall never forget it. From now on, in moments of excessive solitude, I need merely recall those sounds to have the sense of belonging to a community.

§

From the moment defeat was in sight, Hitler spoke of nothing but victory. He believed in it—he behaved, in any case, as if he believed in it—and remained to the end walled up in his optimism, his faith. Everything was crumbling around him, every day belied his hopes but, persisting in his trust in the impossible, blinding himself as only the incurable can, he had the strength to go on to the end, to invent one horror after the next, and to continue beyond his madness, even beyond his destiny. Which is why we can say of him—of the man who failed so utterly—that he realized himself better than any other mortal.

§

"Après moi le déluge" is the unavowed motto of every person: if we admit that others survive us, it is in the hope that they will be punished for it.

§

A zoologist who observed gorillas in their native habitat was amazed by the uniformity of their life and their vast idleness. Hours and hours without doing anything . . . Was boredom unknown to them?

This is indeed a question raised by a *human,* a busy ape. Far from fleeing monotony, animals crave it, and what they most dread is to see it end. For it ends only to be replaced by fear, the cause of all activity.

Inaction is divine; yet it is against inaction that man has rebelled. Man alone, in nature, is incapable of enduring monotony, man alone wants something to happen at all costs—something, anything. . . . Thereby he shows himself unworthy of his ancestor: the need for novelty is the characteristic of an alienated gorilla.

§

We come closer and closer to the Unbreathable. When we have reached it, that will be the great Day. Alas, we are only on the eve. . . .

§

A nation achieves and retains pre-eminence as long as it accepts conventions which are necessarily clumsy, as long as it is given over to prejudices without regarding them as such. Once it calls them by their name, everything is unmasked, everything is compromised.

To seek to rule, to take a role, to make the law—such things cannot be done without a powerful dose of stupidity: history, in its essence, is *stupid*. . . . It continues, it advances, because the nations liquidate their prejudices one after the other. If they were to be rid of them all at the same time, there would be nothing left but a blessed universal disintegration.

§

One cannot live without motives. I have no motives left, and I am living.

§

I was in perfect health, I felt better than ever. Suddenly I was cold, so cold that I was sure there was no cure for it. What was happening to me? Yet this was not the first time I had been in the grip of such a sensation. But in the past I had endured it without trying to understand. This time I wanted to know, and now. . . . I abandoned one hypothesis after the next: it could not be sickness; not the shadow of a symptom to cling to. What was I to do? I was baffled, incapable of finding even the trace of an explanation, when an idea occurred to me—and this was a real relief—that what I was feeling was merely a version of the great, final cold—that it was simply death exercising, rehearsing. . . .

§

In paradise, objects and beings, assaulted by light from all sides, cast no shadow. Which is to say that they lack reality, like anything that is unbroached by darkness and deserted by death.

§

Our first intuitions are the true ones. What I thought of so many things in my first youth seems to me increasingly right, and after so many detours and distractions, I now come back to it, aggrieved that I could have erected my existence on the ruin of those revelations.

§

I remember a place I have been only if I have had the luck to experience utter misery there.

§

At the street fair, watching a tumbler grimacing, shouting, exhausting himself, I told myself that he was doing his duty, whereas I was evading mine. . . .

§

To manifest oneself, to produce in any realm is the characteristic of a more or less camouflaged fanatic. If we do not regard ourselves as entrusted with a mission, existence is difficult; action, impossible.

§

The certitude that there is no salvation is a form of salvation, in fact it *is* salvation. Starting from here, we might organize our own life as well as construct a philosophy of history: the insoluble as solution, as the only way out. . . .

§

My weaknesses have spoiled my existence, but it is thanks to them that I exist, that I imagine I exist.

§

Man interests me only since he has ceased to believe in himself. While he was in his ascending phase, he deserved no more than indifference. Now he provokes a new sentiment, a special sympathy: *compassionate* horror.

§

For all the superstitions and shackles I have rid myself of, I cannot regard myself as a free man, remote from everything. A mania for desistance, having survived the other passions, refuses to leave me: it torments me, it perseveres, it demands that I continue renouncing, withdrawing. But from what? What is left to reject? I ponder the question. My role is over, my career finished, and yet nothing has changed in my life, I am at the same point in it, I must still desist, still and forever.

12

No position is so false as having understood and still remaining alive.

§

When we consider coldly that portion of duration granted to each of us, it seems equally satisfactory and equally ludicrous, whether it lasts a day or a century.

"I've had my time"—no expression can be uttered more appropriately at any moment of life, including the first.

§

Death is the providence of those who will have had the taste and the talent for fiasco—the recompense of all who have come to nothing, who wanted not to. . . . It warrants them, it is their way of winning. On the other hand, for the others, those who have labored to succeed, and who have succeeded: what a denial, what a slap in the face!

§

An Egyptian monk, after fifteen years of complete solitude, received a packet of letters from his family and friends. He did not open them, he flung them into the fire in order to escape the assault of memory. We cannot sustain communion with ourself and our thoughts if we allow ghosts to appear, to prevail. The *desert* signifies not so much a new life as the death of the past: at last we have escaped our own history. In society, no less than in the Thebaid, the letters we write, and those we receive, testify to the fact that we are in chains, that we have broken none of the bonds, that we are merely slaves and deserve to be so.

§

A little patience and the moment will come when nothing more will be possible, when humanity, thrown back on itself, cannot take a single step in any direction. Though we may manage a general sense of this unprecedented spectacle, we should like *details.* . . . And we are afraid we will miss the festivities, not being young enough to have the luck to attend.

§

Whether it is spoken by a grocer or a philosopher, the word *being,* apparently so rich, so tempting, so charged with significance, in fact means nothing at all; incredible that a man in his right mind can use it on any occasion whatever.

§

Getting up in the middle of the night, I walked around my room with the certainty of being chosen and criminal, a double privilege natural to the sleepless, revolting or incomprehensible for the captives of daytime logic.

§

It is not given to everyone to have had an unhappy childhood. Mine was much more than happy—it was *crowned.* I cannot find a better adjective to designate what was triumphant about even its pangs. That had to be paid for, that could not go unpunished.

§

If I am so fond of Dostoevsky's correspondence, it is because he speaks in it of nothing but sickness and money, the only "burning" subjects. All the rest is merely flourishes and chaff.

§

In five hundred thousand years, it appears that England will be entirely submerged. If I were an Englishman I should lay down my arms at once.

Each of us has his unit of time. For one it is the day, the week, the month, or the year; for another, it is a decade, or a century. . . . These units, still on the human scale, are compatible with any plan, any task.

There are some, however, who take time itself for their unit, and sometimes raise themselves above it: for them, what task, what plan deserves to be taken seriously? A man who sees too far, who is contemporary with the *whole* future, can no longer act or even move. . . .

§

An obsession with the precarious accompanies me in every circumstance: mailing a letter this morning, I told myself it was addressed to a *mortal*.

§

One absolute experience, apropos of anything, and you seem, in your own eyes, a survivor.

§

I have always lived with the awareness of the impossibility of living. And what has made existence endurable to me is my curiosity as to how I would get from one minute, one day, one year to the next.

§

The first condition for becoming a saint is to love bores, to endure *visits*. . . .

§

To shake people up, to wake them from their sleep, while knowing you are committing a crime and that it would be a thousand times better to leave them alone, since when they wake, too, you have nothing to offer them. . . .

§

Port-Royal. In that green vale, so many conflicts and lacerations on account of a few bagatelles! Any belief, after a certain time, seems gratuitous and incomprehensible, as does the counter-belief which has destroyed it. Only the stupefaction which both provoke remains.

§

A poor wretch who *feels* time, who is its victim, its martyr, who experiences nothing else, who *is* time at each moment, knows what a metaphysician or a poet divines only by grace of a collapse or a miracle.

§

Those inner rumblings which come to nothing, and by which we are reduced to the state of a grotesque volcano.

§

Each time I am gripped by a fit of rage, I begin by being aggrieved and disgusted, then I tell myself: what luck, what a windfall! I am still alive, I am still one of those flesh-and-blood ghosts. . . .

§

There was no end to the telegram I had just received. All my pretentions, all my inadequacies were in it. Certain failings I myself scarcely suspected were revealed, were proclaimed! What prescience, and what detail! At the end of the interminable indictment, no clue, no trace that permitted me to identify the sender. Who could it be? And why this haste, this unaccustomed means of communication? Who ever spoke his mind with such rigor in his grievance? Where did he come from, this omniscient judge who dared not name himself, this coward in possession of all my secrets, this inquisitor who allowed no extenuating circumstances, not even the ones granted by the most hardened torturers? I too might have made a misstep or two, I too am entitled to some indulgence. I cringe before the inventory of my defects, I choke, I cannot bear this procession of truths. . . . Cursed telegram—I tear it up, and awaken. . . .

§

To have opinions is inevitable, is natural; to have convictions is less so. Each time I meet someone who has convictions, I wonder what intellectual vice, what flaw has caused him to acquire such a thing. However legitimate this question, my habit of raising it spoils the pleasure of conversation for me, gives me a bad conscience, makes me hateful in my own eyes.

§

Once upon a time writing seemed important to me. Of all my superstitions, this one seems the most compromising and the most incomprehensible.

§

I have abused the word *disgust*. But what other can I use to indicate a state in which exasperation is continually corrected by lassitude, and lassitude by exasperation?

§

All evening, having tried to define him, we reviewed all the euphemisms which allow us not to pronounce, in his regard, the word *perfidy*. He is not perfidious, he is merely tortuous, diabolically tortuous, and at the same time innocent, naïve, even angelic. Imagine, if you can, a mixture of Aliosha and Smerdyakov.

§

When you no longer believe in yourself, you stop producing or struggling, you even stop raising questions or answering them, whereas it is the contrary which should have occurred, since it is precisely at this moment that, being free of all bonds, you are likely to grasp the truth, discern what is real and what is not. But once your belief in your own role, or your own lot, has dried up, you become incurious about everything else, even the "truth," though you are closer to it than ever before.

§

In Paradise, I would not last a "season" or even a day; then how account for my nostalgia for it? I don't account for it, it has inhabited me always, it was part of me before I was.

[204]

§

Anyone may now and then have the sense of occupying only a point and a moment; to have such a sense day and night, hour by hour, is less frequent, and it is from this experience, this datum, that one turns toward nirvana or sarcasm—or toward both at once.

§

Although I have sworn never to sin against blessed concision, I am still in complicity with words, and if I am seduced by silence I dare not enter it, I merely prowl on its peripheries.

§

We should establish a religion's degree of truth according to what it makes of the Devil: the more eminent the rank it accords him, the more it testifies that it is concerned with reality, that it rejects deceit and lies, that it is serious, that it sets more store by verification than by distraction or consolation.

§

Nothing deserves to be undone, doubtless because nothing deserved to be done. Hence we become detached from everything, from the original as well as from the ultimate, from advent as well as from collapse.

§

We know, we feel that everything has been said, that there is nothing left to say. But we feel less that this truth affords language a strange, even unsettling status which redeems it. Words are ultimately saved because they have ceased living.

§

The enormous good and the enormous harm I have drawn from my ruminations on the condition of the dead.

§

The undeniable advantage of growing old is to be able to observe at close range the slow and methodical degradation of our organs; they are all beginning to go, some obviously, others discreetly. They become detached from the body, as the body becomes detached from us: it escapes us, flees us, no longer belongs to us. It is a traitor we cannot even denounce, since it stops nowhere and puts itself in no one's service.

§

I never tire of reading about the hermits, preferably about those said to be "weary of seeking God." I am dazzled by the failures of the Desert.

§

If, somehow, Rimbaud had been able to go on (as likely as imagining the day after the apocalypse, or a Nietzsche scribbling away after *Ecce Homo*), he would have ended by reining in, calming down, by glossing his own explosions, explicating them—and himself. A sacrilege in every case, excess of consciousness being only a form of profanation.

§

I have followed only one idea all the way—the idea that everything man achieves necessarily turns against him. The idea is not a new one, but I have *lived* it with a power of conviction, a desperation which no fanaticism, no delirium has ever approached. There is no martyrdom, no dishonor I would not suffer for it, and I would exchange it for no other truth, no other revelation.

§

To go still further than Buddha, to raise oneself above nirvana, to learn to do without it . . . , to be stopped by nothing, not even by the notion of deliverance, regarding it as a mere way-station, an embarrassment, an eclipse . . .

§

My weakness for doomed dynasties, for decaying empires, for the Montezumas of forever, for those who believe in signs, for the lacerated and pursued, for the drunkards of the ineluctable, for the jeopardized, the devoured, for all who are waiting for their executioner . . .

§

I pass without stopping at the grave of that critic whose vitriolic remarks I have so often pondered. Nor at the grave of the poet who spent his life dreaming of his ultimate dissolution. Other names pursue me, alien names linked to a pitiless and pacifying wisdom, to a vision calculated to free the mind from all obsessions, even funereal ones. Nagarjuna, Chandrakirti, Santideva—unparalleled swashbucklers, dialecticians belabored by the obsession of salvation, acrobats and apostles of Vacuity . . . , for whom, sages among the sages, the universe was only a word. . . .

§

No matter how many autumns I observe the spectacle of these leaves so eager to fall, it still surprises me each time—a surprise in which "a chill down the spine" would prevail were it not for the last-minute explosion of a gaiety whose origin I cannot account for.

§

There are certain moments when, remote as we are from any faith, we can conceive of only God as our interlocutor. To address ourselves elsewhere seems an impossibility, a madness. Solitude, in its extreme reaches, requires a form of conversation, also extreme.

§

Man gives off a special odor: of all the animals, he alone smells of the corpse.

§

The hours would not pass; dawn seemed remote, inconceivable. Actually it was not dawn I was waiting for but oblivion of those refractory hours which refused to stir. Lucky the man condemned to death, I told myself, who on the eve of his execution is at least sure of having one good night!

§

Will I be able to stand another minute? will I collapse? If there is one *interesting* sensation, it is the one which gives us the foretaste of epilepsy.

§

A man who survives himself despises himself without acknowledging as much, sometimes without even knowing as much.

§

When you live past the age of rebellion, and you still rebel, you seem to yourself a kind of senile Lucifer.

§

If we did not bear the stigmata of life, how easy it would be to steal away, and how well everything would go by itself!

§

Better than anyone I am able to forgive on the spot. My desire for revenge comes late, too late, when memory of the offense is fading and when, the incitation to action having become virtually nonexistent, I have only one recourse: to deplore my "good feelings."

§

Only to the degree that our moments afford us some contact with death do we have some chance to glimpse on what insanity all existence is based.

§

Ultimately, it is entirely a matter of indifference whether we are something, even if we are God. On this, with a little pressure, almost everyone might be brought to agree. But how does it happen then that everyone aspires to further life, to additional being, and that there is no one who strives to sink, to descend toward the ideal default?

§

According to a belief rather widespread among certain tribes, the dead speak the same language as the living, except that for them words have a meaning contrary to the one they had: large means small, near far, black white. . . .

Does dying come down to that? Still, better than any funereal invention, this complete reversal of language indicates what is unwonted, dumbfounding about death. . . .

§

I am perfectly willing to believe in man's future, but how is one to manage it when still, after all, in possession of one's faculties? It would take their virtually complete collapse, and even then . . . !

§

A thought which is not secretly stamped by fatality is interchangeable, worthless, is merely thought. . . .

§

In Turin, at the beginning of his madness, Nietzsche would rush to his mirror, look at himself, turn away, look again. In the train that was taking him to Basel, the one thing he always asked for was a mirror. He no longer knew who he was, kept looking for himself, and this man, so eager to protect his identity, so thirsty for himself, had no instrument at hand but the clumsiest, the most lamentable of expedients.

§

No one more useless, and more unusable, than I: a datum I must quite simply accept, without taking any pride in the fact whatever. So long as this is not the case, the consciousness of my uselessness will serve for nothing.

§

Whatever the nightmare, one takes a role in it, one is the protagonist, one is something. It is at night that the disinherited man triumphs. If we were to suppress bad dreams, there would be mass revolutions.

§

Terror of the future is always grafted onto the *desire* to experience that terror.

§

Suddenly I was alone with . . . I felt, that afternoon of my childhood, that a very serious event had just occurred. It was my first awakening, the first indication, the premonitory sign of consciousness. Before that I had been only a *being*. From that moment, I was more and less than that. Each *self* begins with a rift and a revelation.

§

Birth and chain are synonyms. To see the light of day, to see shackles . . .

§

To say "Everything is illusory" is to court illusion, to accord it a high degree of reality, the highest in fact, whereas on the contrary one wanted to discredit it. The solution? To stop proclaiming or denouncing it, serving it by thinking about it. The very idea that disqualifies all ideas is a fetter.

§

If we could sleep twenty-four hours a day, we would soon return to the primordial slime, the beatitude of that perfect torpor before Genesis—the dream of every consciousness sick of itself.

§

Not to be born is undoubtedly the best plan of all. Unfortunately it is within no one's reach.

§

No one has loved this world more than I, and yet if it had been offered to me, even as a child, on a platter, I should have shrieked, "Too late, too late!"

§

"What's wrong—what's the matter with you?" Nothing, nothing's the matter, I've merely taken a leap outside my fate, and now I don't know where to turn, what to run for. . . .